# Integrating Theology, Church, and Ministry in a Chinese Seminary

# Integrating Theology, Church, and Ministry in a Chinese Seminary

EDITED BY
PETER L. H. TIE
AND KEVIN S. CHEN

WIPF & STOCK · Eugene, Oregon

INTEGRATING THEOLOGY, CHURCH, AND MINISTRY IN A CHINESE SEMINARY

Copyright © 2024 Wipf and Stock Publishers. All rights reserved. Except for brief quotations in critical publications or reviews, no part of this book may be reproduced in any manner without prior written permission from the publisher. Write: Permissions, Wipf and Stock Publishers, 199 W. 8th Ave., Suite 3, Eugene, OR 97401.

Wipf & Stock
An Imprint of Wipf and Stock Publishers
199 W. 8th Ave., Suite 3
Eugene, OR 97401

www.wipfandstock.com

PAPERBACK ISBN: 979-8-3852-2970-3
HARDCOVER ISBN: 979-8-3852-2971-0
EBOOK ISBN: 979-8-3852-2972-7

10/01/24

Where noted, Scriptures are from Aramaic Bible in Plain English, The Peshitta Holy Bible Translated. Translated by Glenn David Bauscher. Copyright © 2018 Lulu Publishing

Where noted, Scriptures are from The Christian Standard Bible. Copyright © 2017 by Holman Bible Publishers. Used by permission. All rights reserved.

Where noted, Scriptures are from Chinese Union Version with New Punctuation ©1988, 1989, 1996 United Bible Societies. Hong Kong Bible Society.

Where noted, Scriptures are from The ESV® Bible (The Holy Bible, English Standard Version®). ESV® Text Edition: 2016. Copyright © 2001 by Crossway, a publishing ministry of Good News Publishers. The ESV® text has been reproduced in cooperation with and by permission of Good News Publishers. All rights reserved.

Where noted, Scriptures are from GOD'S WORD®, a copyrighted work of God's Word to the Nations. Quotations are used by permission. Copyright 1995 by God's Word to the Nations. All rights reserved.

Where noted, Scriptures are from New American Standard Bible®, Copyright © 1960, 1971, 1977, 1995, 2020 by The Lockman Foundation. All rights reserved.

Where noted, Scriptures are from NET Bible® copyright ©1996-2017 All rights reserved. Build 30170414 by Biblical Studies Press, L.L.C.

Where noted, Scriptures are from THE HOLY BIBLE, NEW INTERNATIONAL VERSION®, NIV® Copyright © 1973, 1978, 1984, 2011 by Biblica, Inc.® Used by permission. All rights reserved worldwide.

Where noted, Scriptures are from the New Revised Standard Version Updated Edition. Copyright © 2021 National Council of Churches of Christ in the United States of America. Used by permission. All rights reserved worldwide.

Where noted, Scriptures are from Revised Chinese Union Version © 2006, 2010 Hong Kong Bible Society.

Peter Tie dedicates this book to his late grandmother, Hung Chong Lau, whose sincere faith made a great impact in him in his childhood (2 Tim 1:5).

Kevin Chen dedicates this book to his parents, Roy and Ellen Chen, who indirectly paved the way for this book through their example of lifelong learning and willingness to cross cultures.

# Contents

| | |
|---|---|
| *Introduction* | ix |
| Developing a Theological Worldview: Seeking to Connect Life, Church, Education, and Ministry<br>DAVID S. DOCKERY | 1 |
| Integration of Faith, Learning, and Ministry: From Union University to Chinese Theological Education<br>KEVIN S. CHEN | 20 |
| Truth, Being True, and Theological Education<br>ESTHER NG | 43 |
| Faith, Knowledge of "the Faith," and a Journey of Faith<br>KENNY LAI | 61 |
| "Your Heavenly Father Is Perfect": Reading the Sermon on the Mount alongside Confucius's *Analects*<br>CHRISTOPHER CHEN | 77 |
| A Threefold Theological Interpretation and a Threefold Practical Implication of the "Spirit" (*pneuma*) in "The Spirit Is Willing, but the Flesh Is Weak" (Matt 26:41b)<br>PETER L. H. TIE | 101 |

# Introduction

WHAT MAKES AN EFFECTIVE seminary education? A perusal of seminary websites for their mission statements shows that student attainment of biblical-theological knowledge, ministerial skills, and character formation are common goals for such institutions. Granting that theological education broadly conceived is also part of the church's regular ministry (e.g., sermons, Sunday school, and sometimes more),[1] achieving these goals for seminaries has many challenges, such as cost, accessibility, preventing theological drift, developing and maintaining church relations, and the need for qualified faculty in some contexts. Among these, a major challenge to seminaries is the relevance of their training to the ministerial contexts of their graduates, whether the church, mission field, parachurch organization, or otherwise. For contexts where theological education is less developed, cultural differences with the West, which has shaped theological education as it stands, make the challenge of relevance even greater. Though not always a bad thing, curriculums and the respective histories of each theological discipline frequently bear a Western stamp. Furthermore, the training of faculty members, even if they are from these developing contexts, often has been similarly influenced, and many books and other materials are translated from English.

The challenge of relevance for a seminary can also be characterized as a challenge of *integration*. In other words, does what I learn in seminary integrate with my life, ministry, and cultural background? Or is seminary education really just a rite of passage that many ministers must go through in order to serve in higher positions in the church? Does theology relate and connect to church ministry, and if so, how? Or, is going to seminary

1. González, "There's No Theological Education."

## Introduction

merely a formality, a going through the motions? What about those who never went to seminary and have become outstanding ministers, even heroes of faith? What about those who did go to seminary, and in some cases excelled, yet who turned out to be failures? In other words, does seminary matter?

As other like-minded seminaries have done, the faculty at our institution have wrestled with these questions over the course of our fifty-year history. As the first Chinese seminary in North America and one of the few freestanding ATS-accredited Chinese seminaries, Christian Witness Theological Seminary (CWTS) and its faculty are constantly trying to integrate (1) rigorous theological education, (2) effective ministerial training for Chinese contexts and beyond, (3) Christian character development for those from a Chinese background, and (4) cultural awareness of traditional Chinese culture, diaspora Chinese culture, and American culture. CWTS serves international students mostly from China as well as diaspora Chinese who have already lived in the US for varying amounts of time. Most of the latter live in Silicon Valley where the seminary is located. CWTS is an interdenominational, conservative evangelical seminary with numerous relationships with Chinese churches, especially in our area.

In line with the objective of effective theological education, the theme of our first Daniel M. Tan Lectureship in 2021 was the integration of theology, church, and ministry. We were privileged to have as our plenary speaker Dr. David S. Dockery, a major figure in Christian higher education and the integration of faith, learning, and more. In addition to two plenary addresses, there were four workshops led by CWTS faculty. Accordingly, the first article in this volume is a programmatic article by Dockery that lays biblical, theological, historical, and practical groundwork for the integration of life, church, education, and ministry (see below for article summaries). Of the four workshops, three were developed into articles in this book (i.e., those by Kevin Chen, Esther Ng, and Peter Tie). Separate from this event, another faculty member, Kenny Lai, has contributed an article, and one more article from an external contributor, Chris Chen, has also been included.

Besides Dockery, all contributors are heavily invested in the work of Chinese theological education. All CWTS faculty contributors hold PhDs in their respective theological disciplines. Many years, even decades, of labor are represented by these authors. These faculty perspectives encompass not only extensive teaching experience and individual research interests

## Introduction

but also administrative experience and significant time mentoring students in our smaller, tightly knit seminary community. The contributors represent life experience in the United States, Taiwan, Malaysia, Hong Kong, the United Kingdom, and Australia. We are all ethnically Chinese and trained in Western theological institutions and yet write from a distinctly Chinese perspective in the spirit of the integrative theological vision that Dockery sets forth. The article summaries below provide an overview of the contents of the book and specific ways that a broader vision for integration can play out specifically in a Chinese cultural context.

As a respected leader in Christian higher education and leading advocate for the integration of faith and learning, David Dockery sets the stage in his article, "Developing a Theological Worldview: Seeking to Connect Life, Church, Education, and Ministry." Rather than seeing the Christian faith as merely concerned with inward, personal piety, Dockery calls for the intentional formation of a theological worldview that encompasses all of life and hence brings together Christian living, church ministry, theological study, cultural engagement, and more. He characterizes this unifying theological vision as being founded on Scripture, Christ-centered, church-focused, and engaged with culture and society. Dockery's article sets forth hopeful possibilities for greater integration that flows from such a theological worldview. Within this broader framework, the rest of the articles in this volume can be seen as contextualizing this vision in various ways for Chinese people.

In "Integration of Faith, Learning, and Ministry: From Union University to Chinese Theological Education," Kevin Chen shows how such integration is important to both an English-speaking, Christian university in the American "Bible Belt" and a Mandarin-speaking Chinese seminary, but applies differently in distinct cultural contexts. Based on firsthand experience and Dockery's *Renewing Minds*, Chen first explains how the vision for the integration of faith and learning impacted his time at Union University, which Dockery led for eighteen years and where he implemented his vision. Chen then discusses challenges to integration in Chinese theological seminaries, especially the strong dichotomy between what is considered "spiritual" and "practical" on the one hand, and "intellectual" and "academic" on the other. He analyzes some of the cultural and historical influences involved and also gives ideas for constructive engagement.

In the current world where scams, lies, and half-truths continue to proliferate, Esther Ng addresses the problem, even crisis, of truth and

## Introduction

sincerity in "Truth, Being True, and Theological Education." On the one hand rooting her analysis in biblical terminology (Hebrew *emeth*, Greek *alētheia*), she also connects it to several specific Chinese terms related to truth and sincerity (*zhen li, zhen xiang, zhen shi, zhen cheng*). Ng explains biblical teaching concerning truth, discusses challenges to this teaching (e.g., modernism, postmodernism, cultural trends, distortions of truth by those seeking power), and gives a Christian response to these challenges. In light of all this, she calls seminaries, churches, and other Christian organizations to work together in seeking the truth, telling the truth, and being true to God, the gospel, and one another.

Kenny Lai addresses the important pastoral issue of the relationship between faith and knowledge in the Christian life in "Faith, Knowledge of 'the Faith,' and a Journey of Faith." He points out from recent surveys that a large proportion of Christians have insufficient knowledge of Christian doctrine. Lai compares a Christian's faith to the root of a tree and knowledge to the tree's source of nutrition, such that both faith and knowledge are necessary for healthy Christian living. He shows in detail from the New Testament how faith and knowledge are involved in a Christian's faith journey from beginning to end, including conversion, sanctification, ministry, family life, and cultural engagement. By holding fast to both faith and knowledge, Christians will be able to endure suffering and finish the race well.

In "'Your Heavenly Father Is Perfect': Reading the Sermon on the Mount alongside Confucius's *Analects*," Chris Chen brings Jesus's classic teaching into conversation with one of the great Chinese classical texts. He shows that the Sermon and the *Analects* both emphasize character over public performance and use shame as a positive force for ethical formation. However, these two texts set forth different paths for attaining virtue. Whereas the *Analects* appeals to impersonal transcendental principles (e.g., *tian, li, dao*), the Sermon bases ethics on the personal relationship that disciples have with God as their perfect heavenly Father. Chen sees Jesus's emphasis on the heavenly Father as the key to distinguishing the Sermon from the *Analects*. His article is an example of how to bring Scripture into fruitful dialogue with one of the world's great texts and cultures, while still maintaining and commending the distinctiveness of the Bible and the gospel.

In "A Threefold Theological Interpretation and a Threefold Practical Implication of the 'Spirit' (*pneuma*) in 'The Spirit Is Willing, but the Flesh Is Weak' (Matt 26:41b)," Peter Tie demonstrates how an

# Introduction

anthropological-pneumatological-Christological interpretation informs, and even transforms, one's understanding and application of this well-known statement by Jesus. The traditional interpretation of Matt 26:41 sees a tension between human spirit and flesh. This form of human spirit versus flesh dichotomy is a deeply embedded cultural assumption (whether in the West or in the Orient) that affects one's interpretation of Jesus's statement, even among leading biblical scholars. Tie shows how Jesus's words "the Spirit is willing" reveal the promise, persistence, and power of the Holy Spirit to pray for believers in their weaknesses. Through the lens of theological interpretation that is in line with the foundational principles of scriptural infallibility-inerrancy, dual-authorship, and *sensus plenior*, Tie paves the way for translating the biblical world and worldview into Christian doctrine and discipleship for the church today.

Beginning with a vision for a unifying theological worldview, this volume thus shows how one group of professor-practitioners promote integration in a Chinese context. There is no doubt that even more topics could have been explored, but we humbly offer these articles to readers in hopes that they will stimulate helpful reflection on the integration of theology, church, and ministry in their own contexts.

## BIBLIOGRAPHY

González, Justo L. "There's No Theological Education Pipeline Anymore." *Christian Century*, Dec. 30, 2020. https://www.christiancentury.org/article/how-my-mind-has-changed/there-s-no-theological-education-pipeline-anymore.

# Developing a Theological Worldview

## Seeking to Connect Life, Church, Education, and Ministry

### David S. Dockery

CHALLENGES ABOUND FOR THE church as well as in the world of Christian higher education in the twenty-first century.[1] Today there are more challenges from more different directions than I have ever seen. Anyone interested in these matters will want to keep an eye on cultural and global trends, for our work never takes place in a vacuum.[2] These introductory observations do not begin to address changes in higher education such as focus, funding, philosophy, methodology, and delivery systems. The list of challenges is lengthy, including legal, cultural, governmental, denominational, financial, and more.[3] Today, however, I want to address a big-picture issue that moves to the very heart of the mission of the church and theological education.[4]

---

1. Portions of this address have been previously published in Dockery, "Christian Higher Education," 17–37; Dockery, *Theology, Church and Ministry*; Dockery, *Renewing Minds*; and Dockery, "Blending Baptist with Orthodox," 83–100.

2. Dockery, "Toward a Future," 115–20.

3. Dockery, "Christian Higher Education in a Changing," 27–30.

4. While the list of challenges facing higher education is lengthy, the issue of mission faithfulness remains at the top of the list. See Dockery, "Change, Challenge, and Confession," 296–308.

# Integrating Theology, Church, and Ministry in a Chinese Seminary

## INTRODUCTORY OBSERVATIONS WITH A FOCUS ON CHRISTIAN HIGHER EDUCATION AT LARGE

Christian higher education involves a distinctive way of thinking about teaching, learning, scholarship, service, subject matter, student life, administration, and governance that is grounded in the orthodox Christian faith. Our vision for this distinctive approach to higher education is not just about an inward, subjective, and pious Christianity, as important as these commitments may be. Christian educators need to recognize that the Christian faith is more than a framework of warmhearted devotional practices, as vital as these are for our Christian formation. Our appeal is for a more fully orbed and theologically shaped vision for our work that will influence what we believe, how we think, how we teach, how we learn, how we write, how we lead, how we govern, how we engage culture, how we prepare students, how we act, and how we treat one another.[5] We are suggesting that a Christian worldview significantly influences our work as Christian educators.

George Marsden, James Burtchaell, and other capable historians have chronicled the secularization of higher education, lamenting "the loss of the soul" and the "dying of the light" among dozens and dozens of formerly church-related colleges and universities in North America and Western Europe.[6] Often the cause for such abandonment of the Christian faith has been traced to the pursuit of academic prestige and cultural respectability in addition to the pressures felt within a rapidly changing secular and pluralistic context.[7] Some church-related schools, including seminaries, have managed to maintain historic ties and denominational connections, but now the Christian faith has little, if any, meaningful influence on the life and work of these campuses, several of which have become some of the most prestigious institutions in this country and around the world.[8]

---

5. Dockery, *What Does It Mean*.

6. See Marsden, *Soul of the American University*; Burtchaell, *Dying of the Light*; Pelikan, *Idea of the University*; Ringenberg, *Christian College*.

7. See Finn, "Knowing and Loving God," 39–41; Dockery, *Renewing Minds*, 1–17; Howard, *Protestant Theology and the Making*; George, *Clash of Orthodoxies*; also Bloom, *Closing of the American Mind*.

8. See Lockerbie, *Passion for Learning*, 312–40; Gangel and Benson, *Christian Education*, 241–366.

## Developing a Theological Worldview

I want to suggest that one thing which has characterized the drift among these institutions has been a lack of an overarching theological worldview to sustain them and to serve as an anchor and compass for the work.[9]

My proposal is not so much to retrace the history of higher education or of Christian higher education in the West so much as it is to suggest that similar pressures and patterns can now be seen in and among a variety of Christian seminaries, colleges, and universities. At many of these institutions, there is a growing academic reputation with expanding academic offerings, something that we celebrate and something for which we are genuinely grateful. Markers of both piety and Christian activism can be found on these campuses. Yet, beyond these things, we need to seek the meaning of true wisdom and human flourishing.[10]

We offer thanks that Christian educators have seen progress in the faith and learning conversation,[11] in the initial steps regarding worldview formation,[12] and even in efforts to begin to reclaim the Christian intellectual tradition.[13] All of these developments are steps toward the development of a greater awareness of the importance of mission-focused efforts for Christian institutions, which is necessary for the long-term health of the church.[14]

I am convinced that Christian institutions can only be sustained in the days and years ahead with such a vision. We will need to begin to develop and enhance partnerships between and among seminaries, Christian colleges and universities, churches, and parachurch ministries that will help to bridge the divide between siloed disciplines and the insularity that develops around scholarly specializations.

I believe this is a critical time to refocus the meaning and mission of Christian entities in order to understand the distinctive reason for their existence.[15] In this secular age, to borrow a phrase from Charles Taylor,

---

9. I have attempted to make this case in other places. See Dockery, *Renewing Minds*, 124–37; Dockery, *Southern Baptist Consensus*, 134–67.

10. Smith, *Desiring the Kingdom*.

11. See Dockery, *Faith and Learning*.

12. See Dockery and Wax, *CSB Worldview Study Bible*.

13. See the fifteen-volume series Reclaiming the Christian Intellectual Tradition, edited by Dockery.

14. Nathan Finn has provided a most helpful outline for such a project. See "Knowing and Loving God," 39–58. Also see D'Costa, *Theology in the Public Square*; Estep et al., *Theology for Christian Education*.

15. See Henry and Beaty, *Christianity and the Soul*.

a time characterized by spiritual confusion, moral anarchy, polarization, and fragmentation, we need to ask foundational questions about the core confessions of our faith.[16] What then would be involved in the development of a thoroughgoing theological worldview framework for these purposes? Such a vision will have (1) Scripture as its foundation, (2) Christ at its center, (3) the church as its focus, and (4) the influencing of society and culture as a key element of its vision.

We believe that theological worldview thinking can render service to the church and to Christian higher education in multiple ways. It addresses the mind so that we can know the triune God as the revelation of himself to us. It informs and undergirds the mission of the church and Christian institutions, making it vitally important for teaching, for connecting the academy with the church, and for the task of cultural engagement. Such an approach serves as a touchstone for understanding what we believe and for recognizing the principles by which our lives are to be shaped.[17] These beliefs and practices come from serious theological reflection, which also points to ethics.[18] One of the goals of Christian higher education is to guide and enable our students as they seek to live in the world with a lifestyle that issues in glory to God. We must therefore help our students connect the dots to begin to see the implications of a vision for a full-orbed Christian approach to life and ministry. Such necessities touch the heart of the life and mission of the Christian faith. As we begin to take these steps, we need to be aware that there are issues in our heritage that may create difficulties for our proposal.

## CHALLENGES FROM OUR HERITAGE

When we think about the particular challenges flowing from our larger evangelical heritage to engage the culture, to carry forth the best of the Christian intellectual tradition, and to develop a theological vision for church and Christian higher education, we recognize a number of things with which we must come to grips. First, the one-sided emphasis on conversion and piety, which has been at the core of these movements and which remains essential, has, at times, however, stood in the way of sanctified intellectual development and cultural engagement. Second, the emphases

16. See Taylor, *Secular Age*; Smith, *How (Not) to Be Secular*; Hansen, *Our Secular Age*.
17. Dockery, *Renewing Minds*, 126–35.
18. See Cole, "Theological Ethics," 316–31.

## Developing a Theological Worldview

on localism, populism, and activism, all of which have frequently acted to spur renewal and mobilization for ministry, have often carried with it a lack of appreciation for the life of the mind and theological development. Third, the diverse camps and entrepreneurial spirit within our larger evangelical worlds have kept us from appreciating the breadth and depth of the Christian theological tradition through the centuries. We recognize that some pockets of our heritage carry with them an embedded anti-intellectualism which has pushed back against serious theological development and serious academic endeavor. Fourth, while seeking to address some of these challenges in years gone by, a form of liberalism has been adopted, which has brought about a loss of direction for both churches and institutions. Fifth, in response to the rise of liberalism has been the rise of an often misguided and reactionary fundamentalism.[19]

Any attempt to develop a theological worldview for Christian higher education must seek to refocus questions related to how Scripture bears upon the various academic disciplines, how we re-appropriate the best of our evangelical heritage, how we clarify our confessional commitments, and how we engage the academy and the culture in this rapidly changing twenty-first-century context.[20]

## FOUNDATIONAL BELIEFS

We begin with an acknowledgment that we will approach the educational enterprise from the perspective of faith seeking understanding.[21] We will then need to develop a framework to cultivate a holistic orthodoxy based on a high view of Scripture, which is also congruent with the Trinitarian and Christological consensus of the early church.[22] I would suggest that an effort to develop theological worldview commitments will not be able to move forward without confessional convictions, which inform both the core and the boundaries of our work. This, however, does not mean that we should

---

19. Dockery, "Evangelicalism," 3–21; also see McGrath, *Evangelicalism and the Future*; Noll, *Scandal of the Evangelical Mind*. It should, by the way, be noted how Billy Graham attempted to address these things in his work with Carl Henry by seeking to bring together the work of evangelism, the cultivation of piety, the engagement of culture, and the importance of serious Christian thinking. See Dockery, "Just as I Am."

20. Finn, "Knowing and Loving God," 39–50.

21. See Dockery, *What Does It Mean*; also Vanhoozer, *Faith Speaking Understanding*.

22. See Dockery, "So Many Denominations," 24–31.

expect or demand uniformity of belief or conviction.[23] The world in which we live with its emphasis on diversity and plurality may well be a creative setting for us once again to pray for a far-reaching renewal of Christian higher education. Our first steps will involve an articulation of foundational commitments, followed by an overview of the early church tradition that will form a framework for this effort.[24] Commitments to the fully truthful and authoritative Scriptures need also to be foundational for our work.[25]

Our approach must be framed by an understanding of the self-revealing God who has created humans in his image. We believe that students created in the image of God and enabled by God's Spirit are designed to discover truth and that the exploration of truth is possible because the universe, as created by the Trinitarian God, is intelligible.[26] At the same time we want to affirm that human beings find their ultimate fulfillment in God, who, though knowable, can never be exhausted or fully known.[27] We will also need a fresh recognition that Christian truth should be the primary authority for both the church and the academic enterprise.[28]

With the apostle Paul, we want to emphasize the Christ-centered approach to developing such a vision. In Eph 4:21, we are reminded that "you heard him [Christ] and were taught by Him, because the truth is in Jesus." In many ways we recognize that Jesus Christ is not only the subject matter in our educational pursuits, but he is also the teacher and the context in which the teaching takes place.[29]

## LEARNING FROM THE CHRISTIAN TRADITION

We therefore want to center our work on Jesus Christ and in the confession that Jesus is Lord, as well as in the great tradition flowing from the Apostles'

---

23. See Erickson, *Evangelical Left*, 131–47; Carson, *Gagging of God*, 480–81; Mohler, "Reformist Evangelicalism," 146.

24. See Oden, *After Modernity*; Oden, *Rebirth of Orthodoxy*, 22–40.

25. See Woodbridge, "Authority of Holy Scripture," 59–80.

26. See Kilner, "Made in the Image," 101–19; Kilner, *Dignity and Destiny*.

27. See Thoennes, "Incomprehensibility of God," 2509–10; also Wilkins and Thoennes, *Biblical and Theological Studies*, 85–109.

28. Dockery, "Christian Higher Education," 17–37; Finn, "Knowing and Loving God," 39–58; Woodbridge, "Authority of Holy Scripture," 59–79; Guthrie, "Study of Holy Scripture," 81–100.

29. Dockery, *Ephesians*, 82–84; Dockery, "Outline of Paul's View," 327–39; Stott, *God's New Society*, 179–83.

## Developing a Theological Worldview

Creed to the confession of Nicea in the fourth century and Chalcedon in the middle of the fifth century. Such historic confessions can provide guidance for us in seeking to balance the mandates for right Christian thinking, right Christian believing, and right Christian living.[30]

When we contend today that church ministry and Christian higher education must both be distinctively Christ-centered, we are in effect confessing that Jesus Christ, who was eternally the second person of the Trinity, sharing all the divine attributes became fully human.[31] Thus, to think of Christ-centeredness only in terms of Christian experience resulting from following certain select teachings of Jesus, while important, will be inadequate. A healthy future for the church and its academic arm must return to the past with the full affirmation that when we point to Jesus, we see the whole man Jesus and say that he is God. This is the great mystery of godliness, God manifested in the flesh (1 Tim 3:16). Our approach to education and ministry is thus significantly shaped and informed by the incarnation.[32]

Such historically grounded confessions can also help us think rightly about faith and about how we relate to one another in love, pointing out the differences between primary, secondary, and tertiary issues in theology and practice. The great confessional tradition, though not the final authoritative word, can serve as a tremendously helpful resource for us in distinguishing primary issues from second and third order doctrines, as well as for providing a safeguard against modern day expressions and echoes of Marcion, Arius, Pelagius, Abelard, and others.[33] We want to learn from the examples of saints and sages who have gone before us, providing images for us of what it means to be ministers and educators who are imitators of Christ.[34]

## THINKING AS WORLDVIEW CHRISTIANS

Theological worldview thinking is certainly not the whole of church and academic life, but there must be a place for a holistic love of God, for Jesus has told us to love God with our heart, soul, strength, *and mind*, and to love our neighbor as well. This should not lead to some cold intellectual

30. Dockery, *Renewing Minds*, 53–69.
31. See Bloesch, *Jesus Christ*.
32. Erickson, *Word Became Flesh*; Noll, *Jesus Christ and the Life*.
33. Dockery and George, *Great Tradition of Christian Thinking*, 51–78.
34. Hood, *Imitating God in Christ*.

approach to the faith unaccompanied by affection.[35] For too many, theology is a kind of intellectual aloofness or an intellectual curiosity lacking heartfelt commitments. But before we can develop a theological worldview framework, we need careful reflection about the meaning of human nature, who we are as ministers, educators, and students, where we stand in the universe, how we think about teaching, learning and service, about goals and tasks, about the place of relationships in community, and about the implications of sin and the meaning of the forgiveness of sins.[36] We must ask what it means for our work as ministers and educators to confess that we believe in "the communion of saints, the forgiveness of sins, the resurrection of the body, and life everlasting."[37] It will also be helpful to think about the relationship of the church to the academy, including an understanding of the responsibility of higher education to prepare future church and denominational leaders.[38]

God's plan for the church is not only central to history but to the gospel and to Christian living as well. We recognize that God is not just saving individuals, he is saving a people for himself. It is vitally important that we understand theological worldview thinking not merely in individualistic terms; we need to also include a corporate and community understanding of these ideas.[39] For these reasons, the early years of Christian higher education placed their focus first in terms of service for the churches and then more broadly for society.[40] We must recognize that those serving in the church and those serving in the academy read different books, listen to different experts, identify different problems, consider different issues, contribute to different journals, and gather in different guilds and societies as they pursue diverse and sometimes competing agendas.[41] Finding ways to reconnect a vision for theology, church, and ministry will be essential for our shared work in the years ahead.

35. See Wolterstorff, *Educating for Shalom*; Holmes, *Fact, Value, and God*; Johnson, *Theology as Discipleship*; Swain, "Godward Mind," 33–36.

36. Dockery, *Renewing Minds*, 87–123.

37. See Packer, *Affirming the Apostles' Creed*; Bird; *What Christians Ought to Believe*; and Mohler, *Apostles' Creed*, 151–205.

38. See Dockery, *Theology, Church, and Ministry*.

39. Though we think that Stanley J. Grenz overemphasized the place of community, there are nevertheless helpful proposals to be found in Grenz, *Theology for the Community*.

40. See the discussions in Brackney, *Congregation and Campus*.

41. See Dockery, *What Does It Mean*; also, Dockery, *Christian Higher Education*, 149–361.

Developing a Theological Worldview

## A FULL-ORBED VISION

We need a theological worldview framework that will help us recover a true understanding of human life. In this sense, we can once again gain a sense of the greatness of the soul. Such thinking can help us recover an awareness that God is more important than we are, that the future life is more important than this one, and that a right view of God gives genuine significance to our academic calling.[42]

Theological worldview thinking can help those who are called to serve both the church and the academy at this time to better understand what they believe and why they believe it. We can all learn to appreciate our heritage and enliven our future hope. When this takes place, many who lack clear direction at the present time will be strengthened. Without the foundation of solid theological thinking, I do not believe there will be effective long-term ministry or educational efforts that are truly and distinctively Christian.

Guided by these basic commitments, theological worldview thinking can help us engage the misdirected thinking often evident in today's academy. An appreciation for our theological heritage and the best of the Christian confessional tradition keeps us from confusing what is merely a contemporary expression from that which is enduringly relevant.[43] Education done with a focus on the church and done for the good of the academy will always have one eye on the best of the Christian tradition.[44]

Knowledge of such continuities and discontinuities in the past will help us focus on the areas of truth that are enduring while encouraging humility as well as dependency on God's Spirit. Hopefully such an awareness will drive us back again and again to the primary source for these worldview commitments, which is Holy Scripture.[45]

Some may wonder if these commitments will stifle honest intellectual exploration. Our challenge will be to preserve faithfully the Christian faith while encouraging serious intellectual inquiry. We believe that these two things can coexist, even if in tension, advancing our shared work in an enriching dialectical dependence.[46]

---

42. See Dockery, "Blending Baptist with Orthodox," 88–92.
43. See Pelikan, *Vindication of Tradition*, 54–56; also Pelikan, *Christian Tradition*.
44. Dockery and George, *Great Tradition of Christian Thinking*, 79–96.
45. See Carson, *Enduring Authority*.
46. Dockery, *Renewing Minds*, 78–90; Dockery, "Christian Higher Education," 27–29.

Guidance and balance in these matters will come as we are faithful in bringing together an informed theological foundation with all areas of learning. This kind of thoughtful integration will enable us to take every thought captive to make it obedient to Christ (2 Cor 10:5) and foster a wholehearted devotion to distinctively Christian thinking, thus helping us to begin to think in a theological worldview fashion across the curriculum. When we begin to grasp the heart of the work of theological education and other aspects of Christian higher education, as well as community service, we will begin to find wisdom to make connections across our fragmented landscape.[47]

## TOWARD A COMPREHENSIVE VISION FOR CHRISTIAN MINISTRY AND EDUCATION

This distinctive approach to life, education, and ministry must offer a way to teach, study, and serve that is consistent with reality by offering a comprehensive understanding of all areas of life and thought.[48] We begin with God, which brings us into his presence without delay. The central affirmation of Scripture is not only that there is a God, but that this God has acted and spoken in history. The triune God is Lord over this world, ruling all things for his glory, displaying his perfections in all that he does in order that humans and angels may adore him.[49] Such thinking provides a coherent way of seeing life, of seeing the world distinct from deism, naturalism, materialism, existentialism, polytheism, pantheism, mysticism, or deconstructionism. Such a God-centered perspective provides bearings and direction when confronted with secularistic and pluralistic approaches to various ideas and issues across the curriculum.

Our twenty-first-century context must once again recognize the importance of serious Christian thinking as necessary and appropriate for the well-being of Christian academic communities. We need an educational vision that is imaginatively compelling, emotionally engaging, aesthetically enhancing, and personally edifying.[50] We believe that the Christian faith, informed by scriptural interpretation, theology, philosophy, and history,

---

47. See the important conversations in Dovre, *Future of Religious Colleges*.

48. See Reynolds, *When Athens Met Jerusalem*.

49. See Carson, *God Who Is There*.

50. Together with more than two dozen other authors, we tried to present such a coherent chorus in the volume titled *Christian Higher Education*.

## Developing a Theological Worldview

has bearing on every subject and academic discipline and on all aspects of life.[51] While at times the Christian's work in the field of education might follow similar methods as the secularists, doxology at both the beginning and ending of one's teaching and research distinguishes the work of believers from that of secularists.[52]

The pursuit of the greater glory of God remains rooted in a Christian way of thinking in which God can be encountered in the search for truth in every discipline. The application of these things will encourage Christian scholars and educators to see their teaching, research, service, and scholarship within the framework of the gospel of Jesus Christ. In these contexts, faithful Christian scholars will be able to see their teaching and their scholarship as contributing to the unity of knowledge.[53] Faculty, staff, and students will work together to enhance a love for learning that encourages a life of worship and service. Such an approach will help us to see more clearly the relationship between the Christian faith and the role of reason, while encouraging Christ followers to seek truth and engage the culture, with a view toward strengthening the church and extending the kingdom of God, including the enhancement of intercultural initiatives and commitments to racial reconciliation.[54]

We are calling for a vision for Christian ministry and education that is unapologetically Christian and intellectually serious. It involves developing resources for serious Christian thinking and scholarship in all disciplines, not just theology, biblical studies, and philosophy. We believe now is the right time to reconsider afresh such a vision, especially with consideration for the challenges and disorder across the academic spectrum and the issues swirling in the church and various denominations.[55] The reality of the fallen world in which we live is magnified for us in day-to-day life through broken families, sexual confusion, abuse, conflicts between the nations, and the racial and ethnic prejudice we observe all around us. This approach to ministry and education will help provide for us a firm grasp of the complexities of the human condition and the natural world.[56]

---

51. See Anthony and Benson, *Exploring the History and Philosophy*.

52. See Noll, "Future of the Religious College," 73–94; Noll, *Jesus Christ and the Life*.

53. See the illustrative chapters in Dockery, *Christian Higher Education*; and Meadors, *Where Wisdom May Found*.

54. See Cha, "Importance of Intercultural," 505–24.

55. See Damrosch, *We Scholars*.

56. See the vision for faithful Christian engagement in Eaton, *Engaging the Culture*.

## Integrating Theology, Church, and Ministry in a Chinese Seminary

This proposal will help us to understand that there is a place for music and the arts because God is the God of creation and beauty.[57] We will encourage scientists to explore the natural sciences in order to contemplate the majesty and greatness of God's creation.[58] We will recognize that the social sciences can make observations to strengthen society, family, and religious structures by recognizing the presence of the image of God in all women and men.[59] Those who study economics will be able to help address problems facing communities and society at large, as well as expand our awareness of how wealth is produced and how good stewardship calls for it to be used.[60] Political-philosophy scholars will thoughtfully strategize about ways to address issues of government, law, public policy, war, justice, and peace. These principles include the dignity of men and women from conception to natural death, the place of marriage and family as foundational for society and the common good, as well as our stewardship of all aspects of this life, from birth to rebirth and beyond.[61] Ethical challenges in business, education, and healthcare can be illuminated by reflection on these truths.[62] This will demand that all of us in both the church and the academy think comprehensively about what it means that God is the source of all truth, all knowledge, and all wisdom, the source of everything that is. The omnirelevance of theological worldview thinking as the creative source in which all creatures live and move and have their being calls for this holistic vision to become a priority for all of us.[63]

Exploring every discipline and approach to our service in the church from a distinctive perspective, which affirms that "we believe in God, the Father Almighty, Maker of heaven and earth," will both shape and sharpen our focus. The more we emphasize the pattern of Christian truth, the more important will its role become for all aspects of life and ministry. This proposal is rooted in the conviction that God, the source of all truth, has revealed himself fully in Jesus Christ (John 1:14–18), and it is in our belief in the union of the divine and human in Jesus Christ that the unity of truth

---

57. See Munson and Drake, *Art and Music*; King, *Beauty of the Lord*.
58. See Bloom, *Natural Sciences*.
59. See Jones, *Psychology*.
60. See Forster, *Economics*.
61. See Baker, *Political Thought*.
62. Mitchell, *Ethics and Moral Reasoning*.
63. See Yarnell, "Systematic Theology," 257–80; Carmody, *Organizing a Christian Mind*, 84–92, 219–23.

## Developing a Theological Worldview

will ultimately be seen. We will need a renewed realization and appreciation of the depth and breadth of this pattern of Christian truth, with its commitments to the church's historic confession of the Trinitarian God, and a recognition of the world and all subject matter as fully understandable only in relation to this Trinitarian God. While our approach to Christian education values and prioritizes the life of the mind, it should be seen simultaneously as a holistic call for the engagement of the head, heart, and hands.[64]

We need to relate to one another in love and humility, bringing about genuine fellowship and community, resulting not only in a rebirth of orthodox foundations but also a renewal of Christian orthopraxy before a watching world.[65] If theological education and Christian higher education entities demonstrated this kind of love and unity, it would do wonders for the larger Christian community. So, the choice is not between theology or ethics, truth or piety, orthodoxy or orthopraxy. The approach we seek is therefore both theoretical and practical. Such a full-orbed and well-rounded vision is not merely about thinking, but also about loving, living, and doing (Matt 22:37–39).

We believe that these commitments are the key for reconnecting theology, education, church, and ministry. Following this path will allow us to see that pragmatic approaches to ministry and education may not be the best way to understand our work, for we will be called to look beyond the horizons that can only be seen from a this-world perspective.

What we are proposing may not be self-evident for some, and these approaches will be challenging for many. It will not be the easiest road to travel, but we believe it provides a faithful path in continuity with the best of the Christian tradition. This proposal offers no room for some vague spirituality to serve as a substitute guide for the work of serious academics. This proposal certainly will require us to think deeply and wrestle seriously with the shaping ideas of history and the challenging issues of our day in the church, in the academy and in the culture, recognizing that the culture and context in which we live and serve has become intrinsically secular. At the same time, we must expand our horizons to help our church members, colleagues, and students appreciate and explore the realities of the global world in which we live and serve, especially in light of what God is doing in and across the Global South at this time. To think otherwise will result

---

64. See Dockery, *Southern Baptist Consensus*, 206–18; Dockery, "Christian Higher Education," 33–37.

65. See Schaeffer, *Church at the End*.

in a generation ill-equipped for faithful service in this century. Instead of allowing our thoughts to be captive to culture, we must take every thought captive to Jesus Christ.

## CONCLUSION

A theological worldview framework for ministry and education will help us develop connecting and unifying principles for Christian thinking, grounded in the truth that God is Creator and Redeemer. We trust that this call will encourage thoughtful exploration and wrestling with the foundational questions of human existence as understood from the vantage point of the Christian gospel. We believe that such a commitment will help us develop a comprehensive and historically informed view of what it means to be a part of the great Christian intellectual tradition as we seek to serve the church and to shape the Christian educational enterprise for the years ahead. We believe that we will be able to encourage others with the confidence that their life, studies, and service are grounded in the reality of the self-revealing God.

This approach will help us to be aware of contemporary cultural, cross-cultural, social, and religious trends. What we are suggesting will require us at times to live in tension in both the church and the academy, reflecting an overarching worldview outlook.[66] Sometimes, however, the issues with which we wrestle will remain filled with ambiguities, which we trust will provide a springboard for lifelong learning and ongoing wrestling with these complex issues.

We would be naïve not to realize that the times in which we live and the context and culture for which our students are preparing to serve will likely push back against this proposal. What will be needed is a bedrock, nonnegotiable commitment to a belief in a triune God—in one mediator between God and humanity, the man Christ Jesus, who was God incarnate.

This commitment represents a belief in a totally truthful and authoritative Bible and in the message of salvation in Jesus Christ by grace through faith. It is rooted in a focus on the church, and it lives in hope of the return of Christ, resulting in a commitment to a life of prayer, holiness, obedience, and growth in Christ.

Faith and courage will be needed for these efforts, commitments that are both firm and loving, clear and gracious. Let us seek to prioritize these

66. See Burtchaell, "Alienation of Christian Higher Education," 129–83.

commitments, which will serve as a guide for us and our students toward lives of faithful discipleship and kingdom living as together we make every effort to keep the unity of the Spirit through the bond of peace (Eph 4:3).

In all of these things we will need to be reminded of our own finitude and sinfulness, which should lead us to fall on our knees in dependence on the triune God who will need to help us and strengthen us by his Spirit for this task if we are to do any good along the way. We are called to seek wisdom, to have our minds opened and ordered, to be oriented toward worship and service, and to trust God for further illumination along these paths.

May God renew the church and the Christian academy as we all seek to develop a framework for these shared efforts. Doing so will not address all or even many of the manifold challenges currently facing the church, the academy, and our culture, but we believe it will indeed help to restore and strengthen the minds, hearts, and hands of God's people, uniting our vision for theology, church, education, and ministry for the years to come.[67] With this hope, let us join together to trust that these shared commitments will not be easily lost or forgotten but will remain firmly rooted in our minds and hearts for years and decades to come for the glory of our great and majestic God.

## BIBLIOGRAPHY

Anthony, Michael J., and Warren S. Benson. *Exploring the History and Philosophy of Christian Education: Principles for the 21st Century*. Grand Rapids: Kregel, 2003.

Baker, Hunter. *Political Thought: A Student's Guide*. Reclaiming the Christian Intellectual Tradition, edited by David S. Dockery. Wheaton, IL: Crossway, 2012.

Bird, Michael F. *What Christians Ought to Believe: An Introduction to Christian Doctrine through the Apostles' Creed*. Grand Rapids, MI: Zondervan, 2016.

Bloesch, Donald G. *Jesus Christ: Savior and Lord*. Christian Foundations. Downers Grove, IL: InterVarsity, 1997.

Bloom, Allan. *The Closing of the American Mind: How Higher Education Has Failed Democracy and Impoverished the Souls of Today's Students*. New York: Simon and Schuster, 1987.

Bloom, John A. *The Natural Sciences: A Student's Guide*. Reclaiming the Christian Intellectual Tradition, edited by David S. Dockery. Wheaton, IL: Crossway, 2015.

Brackney, William H. *Congregation and Campus: Baptists in Higher Education*. Macon, GA: Mercer University Press, 2008.

---

67. See Glanzer et al., *Restoring the Soul*.

# Integrating Theology, Church, and Ministry in a Chinese Seminary

Burtchaell, James Tunstead. "The Alienation of Christian Higher Education." In *Schooling Christians: "Holy Experiments" in American Education*, edited by Stanley Hauerwas and John H. Westerhoff, 129–83. Grand Rapids, MI: Eerdmans, 1992.

———. *The Dying of the Light: The Disengagement of Colleges and Universities from Their Christian Churches*. Grand Rapids, MI: Eerdmans, 1998.

Carmody, Denise Lardner. *Organizing a Christian Mind: A Theology of Higher Education*. Valley Forge, PA: Trinity Press International, 1996.

Carson, D. A., ed. *The Enduring Authority of the Christian Scriptures*. Grand Rapids, MI: Eerdmans, 2016.

———. *The Gagging of God: Christianity Confronts Pluralism*. Grand Rapids, MI: Zondervan, 1996.

———. *The God Who Is There: Finding Your Place in God's Story*. Grand Rapids, MI: Baker, 2010.

Cha, Peter T. "The Importance of Intercultural and International Approaches to Christian Higher Education." In *Christian Higher Education: Faith, Teaching, and Learning in the Evangelical Tradition*, edited by David S. Dockery and Christopher W. Morgan, 505–24. Wheaton, IL: Crossway, 2018.

Cole, Graham A. "Theological Ethics." In *Theology, Church, and Ministry: A Handbook for Theological Education*, edited by David S. Dockery, 316–31. Nashville: B&H Academic, 2017.

Damrosch, David. *We Scholars: Changing the Culture of the University*. Cambridge, MA: Harvard University Press, 1995.

D'Costa, Gavin. *Theology in the Public Square: Church, Academy, and Nation*. Malden, MA: Blackwell, 2005.

Dockery, David S. "Blending Baptist with Orthodox in the Christian University." In *The Future of Baptist Higher Education*, edited by Donald D. Schmeltekopf and Dianna M. Vitanza, 83–100. Waco, TX: Baylor University Press, 2006.

———. "Change, Challenge, and Confession: Looking toward the Future of Christian Higher Education." *Christian Education Journal* 16.2 (Aug. 1, 2019) 296–308.

———. "Christian Higher Education: An Introduction." In *Christian Higher Education: Faith, Teaching, and Learning in the Evangelical Tradition*, edited by David S. Dockery and Christopher W. Morgan, 17–37. Wheaton, IL: Crossway, 2018.

———. *Christian Higher Education: Faith, Teaching, and Learning in the Evangelical Tradition*. Edited by David S. Dockery and Christopher W. Morgan. Wheaton, IL: Crossway, 2018.

———. "Christian Higher Education in a Changing Cultural Landscape: Tradition as a Source for Renewal." *Faith and the Academy* 1.2 (2017) 27–30.

———. *Ephesians: One Body in Christ*. Winter Bible Study, Adult 1997. Nashville: Convention Press, 1996.

———. "Evangelicalism: Past, Present, and Future." *Trinity Journal* 36.1 (Spring 2015) 3–21.

———. *Faith and Learning: A Handbook for Christian Higher Education*. Nashville: B&H Academic, 2012.

———. "Just as I Am: Billy Graham (1918–2018)." Carl F.H. Henry Center for Theological Understanding, Feb. 27, 2018. https://henrycenter.tiu.edu/2018/02/just-as-i-am-billy-graham-1918-2018/.

———. "An Outline of Paul's View of the Spiritual Life: Foundation for an Evangelical Spirituality." *Criswell Theological Review* 3.2 (1989) 327–39.

## Developing a Theological Worldview

———, ed. *Reclaiming the Christian Intellectual Tradition* (series). 15 vols. Wheaton, IL: Crossway, 2012–19.

———. *Renewing Minds: Serving Church and Society through Christian Higher Education.* Nashville: B&H Academic, 2007.

———. "So Many Denominations: The Rise, Decline, and Future of Denominationalism." In *Southern Baptists, Evangelicals, and the Future of Denominationalism*, edited by David S. Dockery, 3–34. Nashville: B&H Academic, 2011.

———. *Southern Baptist Consensus and Renewal: A Biblical, Historical, and Theological Proposal.* Nashville: B&H Academic, 2008.

———, ed. *Theology, Church, and Ministry: A Handbook for Theological Education.* Nashville: B&H Academic, 2017.

———. "Toward a Future for Christian Higher Education: Learning from the Past, Looking to the Future." *Christian Higher Education* 15.1–2 (2016) 115–20.

———. *What Does It Mean to Be a Thoughtful Christian? Questions for Restless Minds.* Bellingham, WA: Lexham, 2022.

Dockery, David S., and Timothy George. *The Great Tradition of Christian Thinking: A Student's Guide.* Reclaiming the Christian Intellectual Tradition, edited by David S. Dockery. Wheaton, IL: Crossway, 2012.

Dockery, David S., and Trevin Wax, eds. *CSB Worldview Study Bible.* Nashville: B&H, 2018.

Dovre, Paul J., ed. *The Future of Religious Colleges: The Proceedings of the Harvard Conference on the Future of Religious Colleges, October 6–7, 2000.* Grand Rapids, MI: Eerdmans, 2002.

Eaton, Philip W. *Engaging the Culture, Changing the World: The Christian University in a Post-Christian World.* Downers Grove, IL: IVP Academic, 2011.

Erickson, Millard J. *The Evangelical Left: Encountering Postconservative Evangelical Theology.* Grand Rapids, MI: Baker, 1997.

———. *The Word Became Flesh.* Grand Rapids, MI: Baker, 1991.

Estep, James R., et al. *A Theology for Christian Education.* Nashville: B&H Academic, 2008.

Finn, Nathan A. "Knowing and Loving God: Toward a Theology of Christian Higher Education." In *Christian Higher Education: Faith, Teaching, and Learning in the Evangelical Tradition*, edited by David S. Dockery and Christopher W. Morgan, 39–58. Wheaton, IL: Crossway, 2018.

Forster, Greg. *Economics: A Student's Guide.* Reclaiming the Christian Intellectual Tradition, edited by David S. Dockery. Wheaton, IL: Crossway, 2019.

Gangel, Kenneth O., and Warren S. Benson. *Christian Education: Its History and Philosophy.* Chicago: Moody, 1983.

George, Robert P. *The Clash of Orthodoxies: Law, Religion, and Morality in Crisis.* Wilmington, DE: ISI Books, 2002.

Glanzer, Perry L., et al. *Restoring the Soul of the University: Unifying Christian Higher Education in a Fragmented Age.* Downers Grove, IL: InterVarsity, 2017.

Grenz, Stanley J. *Theology for the Community of God.* Grand Rapids, MI: Eerdmans, 2000.

Guthrie, George H. "The Study of Holy Scripture and the Work of Christian Higher Education." In *Christian Higher Education: Faith, Teaching, and Learning in the Evangelical Tradition*, edited by David S. Dockery and Christopher W. Morgan, 81–100. Wheaton, IL: Crossway, 2018.

Hansen, Collin, ed. *Our Secular Age: Ten Years of Reading and Applying Charles Taylor.* Deerfield, IL: The Gospel Coalition, 2017.

Henry, Douglas V., and Michael D. Beaty, eds. *Christianity and the Soul of the University: Faith as a Foundation for Intellectual Community*. Grand Rapids, MI: Baker Academic, 2006.

Holmes, Arthur F. *Fact, Value, and God*. Grand Rapids, MI: Eerdmans, 1997.

Hood, Jason B. *Imitating God in Christ: Recapturing a Biblical Pattern*. Downers Grove, IL: InterVarsity, 2013.

Howard, Thomas Albert. *Protestant Theology and the Making of the Modern German University*. Oxford: Oxford University Press, 2006.

Johnson, Keith L. *Theology as Discipleship*. Downers Grove, IL: IVP Academic, 2015.

Jones, Stanton L. *Psychology: A Student's Guide*. Reclaiming the Christian Intellectual Tradition, edited by David S. Dockery. Wheaton, IL: Crossway, 2014.

Kilner, John F. *Dignity and Destiny: Humanity in the Image of God*. Grand Rapids, MI: Eerdmans, 2015.

———. "Made in the Image of God: Implications for Teaching and Learning." In *Christian Higher Education: Faith, Teaching, and Learning in the Evangelical Tradition*, edited by David S. Dockery and Christopher W. Morgan, 101–20. Wheaton, IL: Crossway, 2018.

King, Jonathan. *The Beauty of the Lord: Theology as Aesthetics*. Studies in Historical and Systematic Theology. Bellingham, WA: Lexham, 2018.

Lockerbie, D. Bruce. *A Passion for Learning: The History of Christian Thought on Education*. Chicago: Moody, 1994.

Marsden, George M. *The Soul of the American University: From Protestant Establishment to Established Nonbelief*. New York: Oxford University Press, 1994.

McGrath, Alister. *Evangelicalism and the Future of Christianity*. Downers Grove, IL: InterVarsity, 1995.

Meadors, Edward P., ed. *Where Wisdom May Be Found: The Eternal Purpose of Christian Higher Education*. Eugene, OR: Pickwick, 2019.

Mitchell, C. Ben. *Ethics and Moral Reasoning: A Student's Guide*. Reclaiming the Christian Intellectual Tradition, edited by David S. Dockery. Wheaton, IL: Crossway, 2013.

Mohler, R. Albert, Jr. *The Apostles' Creed: Discovering Authentic Christianity in an Age of Counterfeits*. Nashville: Nelson, 2019.

———. "Reformist Evangelicalism: A Center without a Circumference." In *A Confessing Theology for Postmodern Times*, edited by Michael S. Horton, 131–50. Wheaton, IL: Crossway, 2000.

Munson, Paul Allen, and Joshua Ferris Drake. *Art and Music: A Student's Guide*. Reclaiming the Christian Intellectual Tradition, edited by David S. Dockery. Wheaton, IL: Crossway, 2014.

Noll, Mark A. *Jesus Christ and the Life of the Mind*. Grand Rapids, MI: Eerdmans, 2011.

———. "The Future of the Religious College: Looking Ahead by Looking Back." In *The Future of Religious Colleges: The Proceedings of the Harvard Conference on the Future of Religious Colleges, October 6–7, 2000*, edited by Paul J. Dovre, 73–94. Grand Rapids, MI: Eerdmans, 2002.

———. *The Scandal of the Evangelical Mind*. Grand Rapids, MI: Eerdmans, 1995.

Oden, Thomas C. *After Modernity—What? Agenda for Theology*. Grand Rapids, MI: Zondervan, 1992.

———. *The Rebirth of Orthodoxy: Signs of New Life in Christianity*. San Francisco: HarperSanFrancisco, 2003.

Packer, J. I. *Affirming the Apostles' Creed*. Wheaton, IL: Crossway, 2008.

# Developing a Theological Worldview

Pelikan, Jaroslav. *The Christian Tradition: A History of the Development of Doctrine*. 5 vols. Chicago: University of Chicago Press, 1989.

———. *The Idea of the University: A Reexamination*. New Haven, CT: Yale University Press, 1992.

———. *The Vindication of Tradition*. The 1983 Jefferson Lecture in the Humanities. New Haven, CT: Yale University Press, 1984.

Reynolds, John Mark. *When Athens Met Jerusalem: An Introduction to Classical and Christian Thought*. Downers Grove, IL: InterVarsity, 2009.

Ringenberg, William C. *The Christian College: A History of Protestant Higher Education in America*. 2nd ed. Grand Rapids, MI: Baker Academic, 2006.

Schaeffer, Francis A. *The Church at the End of the Twentieth Century: Including The Church before the Watching World*. Wheaton, IL: Crossway, 1985.

Smith, James K. A. *Desiring the Kingdom: Worship, Worldview, and Cultural Formation*. Cultural Liturgies 1. Grand Rapids, MI: Baker Academic, 2009.

———. *How (Not) to Be Secular: Reading Charles Taylor*. Grand Rapids, MI: Eerdmans, 2014.

Stott, John R. W. *God's New Society: The Message of Ephesians*. The Bible Speaks Today. Downers Grove, IL: InterVarsity, 1979.

Swain, Scott R. "The Godward Mind: An Evangelical Framework for Aspiring to Think Theologically." *Didaktikos* 2.3 (Nov. 2018) 33–36.

Taylor, Charles. *A Secular Age*. Cambridge, MA: Belknap, 2007.

Thoennes, Erik. "The Incomprehensibility of God." In *ESV Study Bible*, edited by Wayne Grudem, 2509–10. Wheaton, IL: Crossway, 2008.

Vanhoozer, Kevin J. *Faith Speaking Understanding: Performing the Drama of Doctrine*. Louisville, KY: Westminster John Knox, 2014.

Wilkins, Michael J., and Erik Thoennes. *Biblical and Theological Studies: A Student's Guide*. Reclaiming the Christian Intellectual Tradition, edited by David S. Dockery. Wheaton, IL: Crossway, 2018.

Wolterstorff, Nicholas. *Educating for Shalom: Essays on Christian Higher Education*. Edited by Clarence W. Joldersma and Gloria Goris Stronks. Grand Rapids, MI: Eerdmans, 2004.

Woodbridge, John D. "The Authority of Holy Scripture: Commitments for Christian Higher Education in the Evangelical Tradition." In *Christian Higher Education: Faith, Teaching, and Learning in the Evangelical Tradition*, edited by David S. Dockery and Christopher W. Morgan, 59–80. Wheaton, IL: Crossway, 2018.

Yarnell, Malcolm. "Systematic Theology." In *Theology, Church, and Ministry: A Handbook for Theological Education*, edited by David S. Dockery, 257–80. Nashville: B&H Academic, 2017.

# Integration of Faith, Learning, and Ministry
## From Union University to Chinese Theological Education

### Kevin S. Chen

THIS PAPER IS DEDICATED to Union University and Christian Witness Theological Seminary (CWTS), two evangelical institutions that I have been privileged to serve as a member of the faculty. It is also within these two very different contexts—one a Southern Baptist liberal arts university in the small, Bible Belt city of Jackson, Tennessee, and the other a Mandarin-speaking Chinese seminary in the large, Silicon Valley city of San Jose, California—that I have had to face the challenges of integrating faith and learning after first learning about it at Union. These experiences spanning fourteen years have been supplemented by various adjunct roles in both English- and Mandarin-speaking contexts. I have found that wrestling with issues of integrating faith and learning in these two very different geographic, cultural, and linguistic contexts have helped me understand such integration better, and I offer this paper in hopes that it will promote conversation about its nature, importance, and challenges in readers' varied contexts.

### INTEGRATION OF FAITH AND LEARNING AT UNION UNIVERSITY

When by God's grace Union University hired me as an assistant professor of biblical studies in 2010, I knew very little about the integration of faith and learning. Taking a step back, I did not even know much about Christian

## Integration of Faith, Learning, and Ministry

colleges and universities, the case for liberal arts, or what it meant to be a faculty member. Jackson, Tennessee, including its own flavor of Southern culture, was also new to me. I had grown up in San Jose, California, and along with everyone I knew, I went to college at public universities or non-Christian private schools. As an engineering major in college, I only took four non-science/engineering courses during my undergraduate studies—quite the opposite of a liberal arts education. Upon arriving at Union, I quickly learned that I had not simply landed at a Christian university but one that was at the forefront of the integration of faith and learning, led by its distinguished then-president Dr. David Dockery, who would serve for a total of eighteen years before moving to Trinity International University/Trinity Evangelical Divinity School and then Southwestern Seminary. Understanding the underlying issues addressed by the effort to integrate faith and learning (i.e., the "why" question) will help us see its relevance for Christian higher education, including theological education, and beyond.

Integration, by definition, involves the bringing together of things that are apart, and the main issues that the integration of faith and learning addresses are the fragmentation of learning across the academic disciplines and for Christians the frequent inability to adequately link study and learning to Christian faith and practice. When I joined the Union faculty, I received a copy of Dockery's *Renewing Minds*, which J. I. Packer called "visionary," "magisterial," and "in every way a landmark book."[1] This book addresses the integration of faith and learning with a fully orbed vision for Christian colleges and universities in particular, although still with relevance to seminaries, Bible colleges, and other institutions.[2] Dockery discusses not only issues related to teaching, learning, and scholarship but also other aspects of university life, including curriculum, trustees, administration, character formation, the university as a Christian community, chapel, the importance of staff, and others.[3] His vision is for "education that is academically rigorous and unapologetically Christian as we seek to become resources for Christian thinking and scholarship in all disciplines for the initial decades of the twenty-first century."[4] In turn, this self-evidently evangelical vision

---

1. Dockery, *Renewing Minds*. Packer's words are part of his endorsement for the book.
2. Dockery, *Renewing Minds*, xvii.
3. Dockery, *Renewing Minds*, 62–66, 73, 87–123.
4. Dockery, *Renewing Minds*, 3. For a related call for cross-fertilization and interdisciplinary thinking with respect to globalization and World Christianity, see the discussion of the "Medici Effect," in Yeh, *Polycentric Missiology*, 54–62.

# Integrating Theology, Church, and Ministry in a Chinese Seminary

is part of Christians' broader calling "to engage [this fallen world] and to sanctify the ongoing secular society in which we live."[5]

Undergirding this impressive vision are fundamental biblical-theological principles. In contrast with the secularization and fragmentation characteristic of academia broadly, Dockery emphasizes Christ's Lordship of all things, including the academic world.[6] In so doing, he follows in the footsteps of James Orr and Abraham Kuyper in the late nineteenth century, Augustine (i.e., "faith seeking understanding"), and many others.[7] Thus, knowledge is not actually disjointed and fragmented but unified, "a seamless whole, because all true knowledge flows from the one Creator to His one creation" and "because all truth has its source in God."[8] Dockery cites supporting biblical passages such as Matt 22:36–40 ("love the Lord your God with all your heart and with all your soul and *with all your mind*"), Prov 1:7 ("the fear of the Lord is the beginning of knowledge"), Rom 12:2 ("be transformed by the renewing of your minds"), and 2 Cor 10:5 ("take captive every thought and make it obedient to Christ").[9] If part of our Christian calling is to love the Lord with all our minds, then "there must be a place for the true intellectual love of God."[10]

These truths enable Christians, especially students and educators, to pursue knowledge as part of their Christian calling and in the context of a unifying Christian worldview. The integration of faith and learning, then, is the opposite of dichotomizing between "the life of the mind and the life of faith."[11] Dockery argues that there is "no room for anti-intellectualism in Christian higher education" and urges us instead to "think Christianly."[12] Christians can even have a "passion for learning based on the supposition that all truth is God's truth."[13] Learning thus can be God-centered as well

---

5. Dockery, *Renewing Minds*, 3. In contrast with fundamentalism, evangelicalism is marked by greater societal engagement.

6. Dockery, *Renewing Minds*, 3–6.

7. Dockery, *Renewing Minds*, 24, 37. Cf. 13, 53–57.

8. Dockery, *Renewing Minds*, 12. The doctrine of common grace is relevant here. See Calvin's *Institutes* II.2.12–17.

9. Dockery, *Renewing Minds*, 8, 12, 45–46.

10. Dockery, *Renewing Minds*, 127. In support of theological education, González, *History of Theological Education*, ix, also cites the Great Commandment (i.e., Matt 22:36–40).

11. Dockery, *Renewing Minds*, 11–12.

12. Dockery, *Renewing Minds*, 46.

13. Dockery, *Renewing Minds*, 47.

## Integration of Faith, Learning, and Ministry

as sought for the sake of serving and edifying others (i.e., love), not simply to satisfy curiosity, wield power, or exalt oneself.[14] Dockery clarifies that his vision "is not just about an inward, subjective, personal, and pious Christianity."[15] This is because faith and learning, Christian commitment and serious study, are "both-ands" not "either-ors."[16] This is a very important point, and Dockery insists, "the choice is not between truth or piety, orthodoxy or orthopraxy . . . it is an attempt to *develop a mind for truth* so that we can articulate the faith once for all delivered to the saints and to *develop a heart for God* so that our lives are built up in the faith."[17] Notice that this statement thoroughly integrates mind, heart, truth, faith, and life.

In contrast with local churches, missions agencies, and other organizations, Dockery reminds us that Christian colleges and universities, though having some overlap in certain aspects, "represent the academic division of the kingdom enterprise" and are "primarily and distinctively academic institutions."[18] Although definitely not ignoring the practical, "Christian higher education does not educate only to serve some practical end" and "must be characterized by delight in learning and teaching, which in turn leads to worship and service."[19] Dockery's vision for the integration of faith and learning gives identity and direction to Christian colleges and universities, even as it still involves Christian living, community life, character formation, and social engagement.[20] As someone who was part of the Union University community for nine years (including the last four years of Dockery's tenure), I had the privilege of experiencing firsthand the outworking of this vision. It thoroughly impacted the institution in the classroom, student life, faculty development, relationships among administration, faculty, staff, and students, and more. This vision was not restricted to the abstract or theoretical but was wisely worked out such that it could be seen, felt, practiced, and enjoyed.

---

14. Dockery, *Renewing Minds*, 49. Dockery cites Bernard of Clairvaux here.

15. Dockery, *Renewing Minds*, 53. On 110, he urges avoidance of "a pietistic form of Christianity that deemphasizes the Christian intellectual tradition."

16. Dockery, *Renewing Minds*, 71.

17. Dockery, *Renewing Minds*, 133. Emphasis original. Cf. 125.

18. Dockery, *Renewing Minds*, 19. Cf. 138–52, where he discusses the strategic role of Christian higher education on the global scene.

19. Dockery, *Renewing Minds*, 110.

20. For the integration of faith and living, see Dockery, *Renewing Minds*, 14.

## INTEGRATION OF FAITH, LEARNING, AND MINISTRY IN CHINESE THEOLOGICAL EDUCATION

### Challenges to Integration for Seminaries Generally

Although less focused on setting forth the unity of knowledge across all academic disciplines, theological education, such as is commonly done in seminaries, faces significant challenges of integration as well. The courses within the curriculum, though certainly valuable in and of themselves, can sometimes feel disjointed and not obviously related to one another. To cite a common example, there can seem to be a gap between Bible and theology courses and ministry or practical theology courses. Oftentimes the real value (and hence purpose) of biblical language courses is also called into question. Do they belong in the curriculum, and if so, to what extent? Within individual disciplines, such as my own (biblical studies), there is also fragmentation resulting from specialization and varied methodologies, with some methodologies even arguing that the biblical material is itself fragmented (e.g., source criticism). These examples involve essentially the same issue of fragmentation discussed above, but limited to seminary coursework.

Perhaps even more pressing is whether seminary studies help (or even hinder) seminary students' personal spiritual growth and how much seminary prepares them practically for ministry. Whereas disjointed courses may be able to be addressed at least partially by better integrating faith and learning (see above), the disconnect between seminary, students' spiritual growth, and ministry must be addressed by an even broader integration of faith, learning, and ministry. In the discussion below, which I intend not as the last word but in hopes of generating further dialogue, I focus on this broader integration.

I begin by acknowledging the pressing importance of students' spiritual growth and the seminary's need to train effective ministers. If, for example, seminary hurts students' spiritual growth, then something is seriously wrong (e.g., the criticism of "seminary" as "cemetery"). When this does happen, the reasons can vary from the seminary itself espousing liberal theology, students being overcommitted such they cannot give enough time to their spiritual health, and/or the seminary failing to sufficiently prioritize and/or attend to the spiritual needs of their students. Likewise, if seminaries are not effectively training ministers for churches and other parachurch organizations, what is the point of investing the time, money, and energy to attend?

Integration of Faith, Learning, and Ministry

## Additional Challenges to Integration for Chinese Seminaries: Misunderstandings and False Dichotomies

These challenges are very real in Chinese Christian circles and (evangelical) Chinese theological education. As we will see below, sometimes these challenges are intertwined with issues specifically related to Chinese culture and/or to Chinese Christians. My colleague Peter Tie has observed some Chinese Christians "strongly discourage seminary studies."[21] Reasons include liberal seminaries (e.g., John Sung's experience at Union Theological Seminary), a privatized notion of the priesthood of all believers (taking the Spirit's anointing in 1 John 2:27 to mean that we don't need seminary), and the ineffectiveness of seminary to produce (enough) quality pastors.[22] In Tie's view, the root problem is not seminary per se but a problem of integration, i.e., "how intentionally and persistently seminaries integrate the two seemingly separate aspects—knowledge and practice, theology and life, Scripture and ministry—into a coherent whole."[23]

Though there definitely are exceptions and I make no attempt to generalize about all Chinese Christians, Chinese evangelicals that I have observed tend to be pietistic and practical.[24] We care deeply about (hard-won) spiritual life (靈命; cf. 生命) and want to learn things that we can immediately use (實際/實踐). As such, Chinese Christians sometimes object to things considered to be overly academic (學術), abstract (抽象), merely theoretical (理論), or just some (useless) knowledge (知識). Tie cites complaints that seminary helps students gain "theological knowledge" but dampens "spiritual passion," and that it is too academic and intellectual and not practical and spiritual enough.[25] The push for practical (and fast) theological education is felt both at CWTS and in other quarters.[26] Certainly, seminaries are not to "quench the Spirit" (1 Thess 5:19), but if the above fairly represents many Chinese evangelicals, then objections to

---

21. Tie, "Spirit, Scripture, Saints," 6.

22. Tie, "Spirit, Scripture, Saints," 6–7.

23. Tie, "Spirit, Scripture, Saints," 8.

24. For discussion of broader attempts to classify Chinese Protestants, see Chow, *Theosis, Sino-Christian Theology*, 3–15. I would like to thank Dr. Chow for interacting with me regarding this issue (and other related ones) and for pointing me to helpful bibliographies not limited to his own work.

25. Tie, "Spirit, Scripture, Saints," 7.

26. Fulton, *China's Urban Christians*, 56, reports that theological education in China faces major pressure to be "pragmatic" and "fast."

## Integrating Theology, Church, and Ministry in a Chinese Seminary

seminary are often based on an either-or conception of spiritual versus intellectual/academic, heart versus mind, practical versus theoretical/theological, knowledge versus passion. Observations concerning Chinese people generally as pragmatic and preferring concrete thinking (e.g., proverbial sayings) rather than theoretical speculation or other more abstract thinking suggest that these objections reflect Chinese culture more broadly.[27]

In the spirit of Dockery's proposal discussed above, I suggest that Chinese Christians rightly care deeply about loving the Lord with all our heart (spiritual) and all our strength (practical) but are sometimes less intentional about loving the Lord with all our mind in all that could entail. This is not to say that Chinese Christians are unconcerned with our thought-life (e.g., sinful thoughts) or that all Christians should become scholars or theologians but rather that faithfulness to the Great Commandment suggests that we can make more room to love the Lord with our minds. The direction this may take and the amount of time invested will vary for each individual based on temperament, gifting, and circumstances, but all Christians are still called to love the Lord with all their beings, including their minds.

An either-or view of spiritual and academic, theoretical and practical, etc., contrasts with Chinese preference for both-and in other situations (i.e., the classic example of Daoism's yin and yang).[28] Another way of characterizing this either-or is that the implied definitions of "spiritual" and "practical" include certain emphases and, with them, exclusions. "Spiritual" (屬靈) seems to refer to a believer's inner communion with God based on the accumulation of their lived experience as a Christian. There are many positive things about this implied definition, such as the priority placed on prayer, faithfulness, and Christian character. Some Chinese seminaries' practice of morning prayer and emphasis on spiritual formation is exemplary, for instance. While affirming these emphases, we suggest that "spiritual" should be defined broadly enough to include obedience to all of God's commands, especially the Great Commandment. As mentioned above, rightly loving the Lord with all our minds results in worship and service, not pride and

---

27. Covell, *Confucius, Buddha, and Christ*, 11.

28. The author has witnessed the difficulty that a group of Chinese people had with the game of "Would You Rather?" because it forced them to make an either-or choice. Likewise, my Chinese students try to explore both-and solutions more often when presented with competing views than American students that I have taught. Of course, Chinese preference for both-and is not absolute (and neither is Western thinking purely either-or). See Yeh, *Polycentric Missiology*, 42, 52; Wan, "Critiquing the Method."

## Integration of Faith, Learning, and Ministry

self-gratification. Surely there is a way to love the Lord with all our minds in concert with other aspects of our Christian calling.

Likewise, the implied definition of "practical" seems to be something that is *immediately* useful and hands-on, even tangible. Learning that can be immediately used has great value of course, but, in reality, the distinction between theoretical and practical is not so hard and fast. There are certainly courses (e.g., preaching, counseling, apologetics, etc.) that are more immediately applicable in ministry, but this does not mean that the others are not "practical."[29] Biblical languages should also be thought of as "practical" in the sense that knowing them greatly helps with understanding and interpreting the Bible, our supreme authority for Christian faith, practice, and ministry. If our faith, life, and ministry are supposed to be deeply rooted in the Scripture, certainly serious study of it can be "practical" (and motivated by love for the Lord and his word). The real issue is more of a cost-benefit issue (i.e., time invested to learn compared to the benefit to a particular learner), which does not exactly correspond to the issue of practicality.

We should remember that there are many things in life worth learning but that take a long time to do so (e.g., foreign languages generally, musical instruments, athletics, medicine and many other professions and trades). Christian living itself is like this. All such things require patience. Even ministry courses, like preaching, are really the beginning of lengthy learning process, even if they can be practiced immediately. There is a sense in which this is also true for the entire seminary curriculum. Seminary education is thus an investment in the future, even as it prepares students as much as possible for ministry upon graduation given their background, degree program, and other factors. Such a perspective contrasts with pursuing seminary education primarily to get certification (i.e., a degree) for the sake of personal advancement and/or because it is required for certain ministry roles.[30] We should also make clear that some "practical" issues necessarily must be learned in a particular local congregation itself, such as how to wisely serve them, which in turn requires getting to know them, building relationships over time, and learning how to work together.

---

29. Sailhamer, "Nature, Purpose, and Tasks," 11, believes that the tension between theoretical and practical in a seminary is only a surface tension because the fundamental task of interpreting and applying Scripture to life is the same across the curriculum.

30. Fulton, *China's Urban Christians*, 37, reports that the desire for "degrees just to get the title" is common in China among both house church and TSPM (Three-Self Patriotic Movement) leaders.

Integrating Theology, Church, and Ministry in a Chinese Seminary

From a historical perspective, González's survey of theological education from the early church to the present also shows us that "practical theology" (or pastoral theology) in a modern sense is often traced to Schleiermacher in the early nineteenth century (his 1811 *Brief Outline of Theological Studies*).[31] Although practical studies had already been part of theological curricula since the Reformation era (e.g., Hyperius, 1511–64), practical theology in Schleiermacher's day coincided with the continued, Enlightenment-driven growth over the next century and beyond of scientific research and knowledge.[32] Eventually, this growth gave rise to new disciplines (e.g., psychology, education, communications, sociology, economics, business management), which in turn resulted in counterparts in practical theology coursework. González comments that this "complicated the theological curriculum" and that these courses (e.g., pastoral counseling, Christian education, homiletics, church management) tended to resemble their secular counterparts and lack sufficient theological reflection.[33] Of course, this need not be the case. My purpose here is not to question the importance of practical theology in the curriculum (which I wholeheartedly affirm) but rather to highlight the necessity of its being deeply rooted in the traditional biblical and theological disciplines, which is what has always made theological education distinctive. González himself recognizes the problem of theological education that is largely irrelevant to ministerial practice and rightly insists that theological education in "its proper place ... is at the heart of the church" and hence seminaries exist for the church, "never above nor apart from it."[34]

## A Different Seminary Identity and Different Historical and Circumstantial Factors

Returning to Chinese seminaries, it should not be surprising that the implied understandings of "spiritual" and "practical" have led to a different

31. González, *History of Theological Education*, 106–7.

32. González, *History of Theological Education*, 74, 107–11. González explains that Hyperius's division of the curriculum into biblical studies, doctrine, and practical studies "was very similar to what eventually most Protestant seminaries would follow" (74).

33. González, *History of Theological Education*, 110; see also 110–11.

34. González, *History of Theological Education*, 127; see also 51, 53. González uses "theological education" in a broad sense and "part of the very essence of the church" through its history (ix), whereas theological education by seminaries has only existed for five hundred years (xi).

## Integration of Faith, Learning, and Ministry

configuration of seminary identity. Whereas many American seminaries seem quite comfortable with their identity as academic institutions with their main accrediting body as the Association of Theological Schools (ATS), Chinese seminaries, while not avoiding "academics" (學術) altogether, strike a different balance between academics, spiritual formation ("spiritual"), and hands-on ministry training ("practical"), with the latter two elevated in importance. My institution, Christian Witness Theological Seminary, celebrated its fiftieth anniversary in 2023 but has only been fully accredited by ATS since 2016 (associate membership in 2004; candidacy for full membership in 2014). It was founded in 1973 essentially as a training center and gained degree-granting privileges from the state of California in 1984.[35] We have come a long way, even as our history as well as the expectations of Chinese churches still have their influence. To cite another example, a local unaccredited seminary enjoyed a strong reputation in Chinese circles for a period of time because of its respected president.[36] Thus, in a constituency where accreditation is less uniform (e.g., ATA [Asia Theological Association] accreditation being yet another option) than for English-language contexts in the United States and Canada (where ATS accreditation is often assumed), the role of and standards for academics, and the lines between an ATS-accredited seminary (or a Chinese program in an English-speaking ATS-accredited seminary), an ATA-accredited seminary, an unaccredited seminary, and a training center are not always obvious. These things are especially true in China where accreditation is more difficult and in some cases not necessarily on the radar.[37] In the end, the role of and standards for academics vary, but the emphasis on the "spiritual" and the "practical" remains.

From what I have seen, the aforementioned implied definitions and dichotomies concerning "spiritual" and "practical" are deeply held, sometimes even seemingly set in stone. These entrenched beliefs correspond to

---

35. Christian Witness Theological Seminary, "Vision Statement." Thank you to Dr. Esther Ng, longtime CWTS faculty member and former academic dean, for confirming this. According to the website, CWTS attained permission in 1984 from "the California Superintendent of Public Instruction to confer bachelor and master [sic] degrees."

36. I.e., John Tsang (曾霖芳) of Overseas Theological Seminary (海外神學院).

37. For an introduction to seminaries in China as of 2003, see Aikman, *Jesus in Beijing*, 119–33. More recently, see Fulton, *China's Urban Christians*, 34–38. From what I know, there can be issues of security and relevance. Cf. the founding of Hunan Bible Institute (a Bible school, not a seminary) as recounted in Xiyi Yao, "Hunan Bible Institute," 126–27, 129–30, 140. In fundamentalist circles, Bible schools outnumbered seminaries (125).

## Integrating Theology, Church, and Ministry in a Chinese Seminary

historical and cultural factors. Beginning with more recent history, representatives of house churches in China (one segment of the Chinese church though not the whole) acknowledged in a 1998 statement their lineage as being from fundamentalists and evangelicals.[38] More broadly, Chow remarks, "the dominant theological orientation of TSPM congregations and house churches is fundamentalism or evangelicalism, emphasizing the depravity of humanity and the need for individual salvation."[39] Insofar as evangelicals and especially fundamentalists more broadly have also struggled with the place of the Christian mind, we should expect that many conservative Chinese Christians would struggle similarly. This is especially true for Chinese house churches, whose relationship to the state is tenuous and complex. To varying degrees, the reality of limited opportunities and access to theological education (whether institutions, personnel, literature, or otherwise) adds to the challenge. Regarding American evangelicals, we may recall Noll's famous criticism, "The scandal of the evangelical mind is that there is not much of an evangelical mind."[40] His chapter "The Intellectual Disaster of Fundamentalism" further chronicles the anti-intellectualism and isolationism of fundamentalism and the formative impact this had on later evangelicals.[41] Yao believes that fundamentalism has "deeply shaped" Chinese Protestants (not just house church Protestants).[42] He cites the example of Hunan Bible Institute (or HBI, 1916–52), which experienced direct fundamentalist influence through formal oversight by Biola.[43]

---

38. Aikman, *Jesus in Beijing*, 323.

39. Chow, *Theosis, Sino-Christian Theology*, 38. In the same context, he also observes, "the majority of Chinese congregations today continue to maintain the conservative type A [i.e., law-oriented] legacy of their predecessors." Kwok, "Sola Scriptura's," 93, likewise asserts that most Chinese Christians are theologically conservative.

40. Noll, *Scandal of the Evangelical Mind*, 3. Ten years later (2004), Noll still held to his basic thesis but was more hopeful. See Noll, "Evangelical Mind Today." See the recent, weighty criticism of Noll (and Marsden) especially in light of the current cultural climate by Trueman, "Failure of Evangelical Elites."

41. Noll, *Scandal of the Evangelical Mind*, 109–45. On 122, he remarks, "The fundamentalist era remains critical for evangelical thinking, since it so thoroughly established habits of mind for looking (or not looking) at the world." Despite evangelicalism's distinctives, it has "largely retained the mentality of fundamentalism *when it comes to looking at the world*" (137, emphasis added).

42. Xiyi Yao, "Hunan Bible Institute," 124.

43. Xiyi Yao, "Hunan Bible Institute," 127, 133–39. He has a very positive assessment of HBI, drawing attention to the balance between academics and practical ministry (130) and its being "more than just a school, but also a powerhouse of church ministry" in Hunan and beyond (132). See 139–40.

## Integration of Faith, Learning, and Ministry

The long-term experience of persecution by house churches in China adds yet another factor. Their leaders have testified of how much they learned through enduring prolonged suffering. As an example from the older generation, the well-known Fangcheng leader Zhang Rongliang (張榮亮) once remarked, "Chinese prison is my seminary . . . Police handcuffs and the electric nightstick are our equipment."[44] Such testimony deservedly commands respect and honor (it will always have mine), and although it does not reject traditional seminary training, some could take it in that way. Certainly, it emphasizes experiential knowledge of God gained through life, especially suffering. At the same time, there have been and still are opportunities for house church leaders to attend seminary.[45]

This tradition emphasizing experiential knowledge of God, along with uncertainty concerning the role of the intellect and academics, can be traced back still further to additional key figures. Tseng comments that Wang Mingdao's preaching and writing ministry was strongly biblical, "but study of the Bible as an academic discipline is not what preoccupies him. Instead, he focuses on the integrity of a Christian's personal life and the church's moral witness to a corrupt society."[46] She further notes the characteristic "plainness," "common sense," and "reasoned and pragmatic application" of Wang's teaching.[47] His approach to understanding the Bible was relatively simple: read it (e.g., book by book starting with the NT, one chapter at a time), pray for the Spirit's help in faith, break the chapter up into sections, understand the main idea of each section, identify key truths or teachings, and memorize key verses.[48]

Kwok describes both Wang's and Watchman Nee's approach to the Bible reading as "mainly a spiritual practice" rather than "an intellectual undertaking."[49] Such reading was focused on "spiritual cultivation" rather than hermeneutical methodology.[50] The spiritual versus intellectual dichotomy implied here contrasts with Dockery's both-and approach

---

44. Aikman, *Jesus in Beijing*, 133. See also Sister Ding's testimony, "It was during my time in prison . . . that the Holy Spirit taught me the most" (104).

45. See n37 above.

46. Tseng, "Revival Preaching and the Indigenization," 179.

47. Tseng, "Revival Preaching and the Indigenization," 179.

48. Kwok, "Sola Scriptura's," 101–2. Cf. Wang, "怎样读圣经?," 61–63. He believed that the whole Bible was filled with important teachings. On 64, he adds that commentaries are unnecessary because Scripture is its own interpreter (i.e., Scripture interprets Scripture).

49. Kwok, "Sola Scriptura's," 100.

50. Kwok, "Sola Scriptura's," 101–2.

described above.[51] For Chinese fundamentalists such as Wang and Nee, their devotion to Scripture was expressed more through its use for spiritual and moral cultivation, unlike their Western fundamentalist counterparts who focused more on doctrinal purity.[52]

## The Influence of Watchman Nee

Nee's ideas on such matters deserve extended treatment. The focus on (a certain form of) spiritual cultivation is especially clear in Nee's insistence that a proper reading of the Bible must first have a proper reader, who is more important than the method: "the person first, then the method [人在先, 方法在後] . . . method is not first, but the person [方法不是第一, 人是第一]."[53] Nee's own testimony in the (first) preface to *The Spiritual Man* (屬靈人) agrees with this, "I felt the urgent need for a book—based on the Word and on experience—which would give God's children a clear understanding of spiritual life."[54] In this preface, he does not clearly distinguish between the relative authority of Scripture and experience, and he cites the Bible as permitting believers to share their experiences as well as the Holy Spirit's leading to do so.[55] After explaining that the writing process for *The Spiritual Man* went on hiatus for three years because his own experience was lacking for the truths he wanted to convey, Nee asserts concerning the final product, "We base everything on the Bible and prove all by spiritual experience."[56]

Especially important for the present purposes, Nee holds to a trichotomous view of human beings. A person is composed of spirit, soul, and body (靈魂體)—in that order, based on 1 Thess 5:23 and analogous to the holy of

---

51. As a broad parallel to such dichotomizing from the same era, Ireland, *John Song*, 80–81, 85, 126, notes that Song's revivalist preaching involved sharp dichotomies as he urged his audience to make a decision.

52. Kwok, "Sola Scriptura's," 102; Wan, "Competing Tensions," 106. On 97, Wan characterizes theological conservative Chen Chonggui as "focused less on understanding the text than on practising what was supposed to be self-evident in the text."

53. 倪柝聲 (Watchman Nee), 讀經之路, 2. Cf. Kwok, "Sola Scriptura's," 101.

54. Nee, *Spiritual Man*, 1:7. Original Chinese version: 倪柝聲, <屬靈人>, from which the original Chinese title and Chinese terms below are taken.

55. Nee, *Spiritual Man*, 1:7.

56. Nee, *Spiritual Man*, 1:11; 8. Cf. 86–87, where he contrasts genuine experience and being taught by "the Holy Spirit Who alone truly teaches us" with fleshly Christians who like the Corinthians who were proud of their knowledge but "all their understandings were in the mind" and "merely a product of the mind."

holies, holy place, and outer court in the temple.[57] For Nee, a person's spirit, which is the means of conscience, intuition (直覺), and communion with God, should rule their mind (心思), which, along with emotion and will, is part of the soul and provides self-consciousness.[58] This sharp distinction between the superior, intuitive "spirit" and the lesser rational mind takes the emphasis on so-called spiritual cultivation to another level through a theological anthropology that subordinates the place of the mind in the person and in the Christian life.[59] Lam has also noticed the division between spirit and mind, along with the latter's subordination, in Nee's theology.[60] Chow has highlighted the importance of theological anthropology in Chinese Christian theology generally, and Lam in particular sees Nee's theology as a "spiritual theology" (屬靈神學) based on his trichotomous anthropology.[61]

For Nee, the intellect and reason is thus on a lower plane than the spiritual. Accordingly, Nee warned against "spiritualizing a rational life" and the "danger" that a believer might go too far in suppressing his soulish emotion and still be soulish, i.e., "a rational [屬理智], not a spiritual, man."[62] Like those who do not wait on God or rely on the Spirit's leading and instead use their mind and books to seek knowledge, Nee casts the fall as "occasioned by seeking knowledge" (從尋求知識來的), asserting, "Intellect was the chief cause of the fall" (perhaps softened from the original: 智力是墮落的原因).[63] Nee's bifurcation of reason and spirit contrasts with Dockery's proposal for integration described above.[64]

---

57. Nee, *Spiritual Man*, 1:28–30.

58. Nee, *Spiritual Man*, 1:31–38, 43, 63. See Nee, *Normal Christian Life*, 224; Chow, *Theosis, Sino-Christian Theology*, 44–47, 50–51; Covell, *Confucius, Buddha, and Christ*, 198.

59. See Nee, *Normal Christian Life*, 226: "The fruit of the tree of knowledge made the first man *overdeveloped in his soul*. The emotion was touched … making him 'desire'; the mind with its reasoning power was developed" (emphasis original). Although Nee does discuss the mind at length in *Spiritual Man*, 3:7–74, he does so from the perspective of combating evil thoughts and temptation. For him, the mind is a "battlefield" with truth on the one side and Satan and evil spirits on the other. Nee even hints at "how much of the world's philosophy, ethics, knowledge, research, and science flow from the power of darkness" (3:9). A believer, however, can attain "a spiritual mind" (3:67).

60. 林榮洪 (Lam), 屬靈神學, 284.

61. Chow, *Theosis, Sino-Christian Theology*, 37–40; Lam, 屬靈神學, 6, 278.

62. Nee, *Spiritual Man*, 1:19.

63. Nee, *Spiritual Man*, 1:47. Despite the mitigating comment, "Although such [i.e., Eve's] searching for knowledge was perfectly legitimate" (1:46), Nee's more negative view of the mind is evident through his other statements.

64. Dockery does not directly engage Nee's trichotomous framework, but we would

## Integrating Theology, Church, and Ministry in a Chinese Seminary

Nee goes on to criticize those who are very intelligent but do not understand the things of the Spirit.⁶⁵ He also taught that the new birth acts on the spirit, not the soul or the body, which are under the power of the flesh.⁶⁶ He remarks, "Many of us Christians today are men with over-developed souls [e.g., minds/brains by implication]. We have grown too big in ourselves."⁶⁷ Furthermore, "without the guidance of the Holy Spirit intellect not only is undependable but also extremely dangerous, because it often confuses right and wrong."⁶⁸ Certainly, Christians would agree that the fall has affected the mind and that we should "lean not on our own understanding" (Prov 3:5) as our highest authority, but Nee's views suppress the place of the mind, which in reality we cannot help but use constantly. Is it really possible to isolate the rule of the spirit operating through conscience, intuition, and communion with God from the working of the soul (mind, emotions, and will)? Moreover, a person's intuitive sense gained from communion with God can be very subjective, as well as difficult to distinguish from feelings and intellect.⁶⁹ Without assuming that all theologically conservative Chinese Christians affirm or are even aware of Nee's theological anthropology, Chow's attention to Nee as well as the following remark suggests Nee's continuing impact, "The tremendous numbers of his direct and indirect followers can attest to the strength of his legacy."⁷⁰

---

not expect this.

65. Nee, *Spiritual Man*, 1:52–53. See Nee, *Normal Christian Life*, 229–33; Chow, *Theosis, Sino-Christian Theology*, 46–47, 51.

66. Nee, *Spiritual Man*, 1:61, 70, respectively. On 70, he writes, "[In the fall,] man became a fleshly, not a spiritual, man. . . . the soul is now under the power of the flesh . . . Whatever is soulical has become fleshly." Further, "the flesh in a saint is the same as that in a sinner. In regeneration [which acts on the spirit] the flesh is not transformed" (76). For immature believers, the flesh is still powerful (81). Consequently, an immature "new believer still walks in the realm of feelings and thoughts [i.e., soul]. . . . A newly born Christian cannot help being fleshly" (84). Nee's view that the fall involved the confusion of the proper order of spirit, soul, body (43–50) has an earlier Keswick parallel. See Hopkins, *Law of Liberty*, 45, where the "carnal" Christian "is no longer spirit, soul, and body, but rather body, soul, and spirit, the order being reversed, the lowest principle becoming dominant." Regarding the creation and fall of man, see *Law of Liberty*, 57–65. He assigns reason to the soul (*Law of Liberty*, 62–63). Regarding the mind of Christ, see *Law of Liberty*, 68–73.

67. Nee, *Normal Christian Life*, 228.

68. Nee, *Spiritual Man*, 1:53.

69. Cf., Lam, 屬靈神學, 282–85.

70. Chow, *Theosis, Sino-Christian Theology*, 63; see 41. Cf. Lam, 屬靈神學, 278. Nee's books continue to be sold at Chinese Christian bookstores, as I saw at Tien Dao

# Integration of Faith, Learning, and Ministry

## Additional Historical Factors

Going back even further, Starr points out that the identity of the Chinese Bible (聖經) as *jing* since the 1830s and 1840s situates it within the canon of Chinese classics and the way these works were read.[71] She explains that the Chinese classics were not just studied for the sake of imperial examinations but "were also the moral and ethical base for Chinese society. Moral and ritual behavior was so codified under the Confucian textual heritage that knowing the texts was seen as equivalent to embodying them: to be a scholar was to have internalized the precepts of the classics."[72] Similarly, Wan contrasts Western hermeneutical theory that presupposes an unbroken reading tradition with the way Chinese Protestants from 1919–49 would have read the (foreign) Bible like a Chinese classic, "for the sake of self-transformation, moral cultivation, discovering ethical injunctions or 'constituting the body and establishing destiny' [安身立命]."[73] In particular, Wan explains that Jia Yuming's theological system of "perfect salvation" (完全救恩; emphasizing Jesus and the cross) is "both a reading strategy [for the Bible] and a programme for spiritual and moral cultivation."[74] This involved a "spiritual interpretation" of Scripture (靈意解經) that followed a spiritualization of one's intellect (理性靈性化), ultimately resulting in spiritual wisdom (靈智).[75] This spiritualization of the intellect is part of the

---

Christian Bookstore (Milpitas, CA) on Jan. 5, 2022.

71. Starr, *Reading Christian Scriptures*, 2.

72. Starr, *Reading Christian Scriptures*, 3.

73. Wan, "Competing Tensions," 98. Ireland, *John Song*, 68, notes that Sung's Republican Era "audiences were eager, like their Buddhist and Daoist neighbors, to penetrate to deeper layers of meaning embedded in a holy text."

74. Wan, "Competing Tensions," 103-4.

75. Wan, "Competing Tensions," 104. Cf. Jia, 完全救法, 1:124-26. On 12, he refers to "the need to read the Bible with spiritual eyes" (要用屬靈的眼光讀聖經). On 167-68, Jia uses the phrase "according to the spiritual meaning" (按靈意) several times to explain the meaning of various colors related to the temple. For a definition of spiritual interpretation, see 梁家麟, <為靈意解經辯誣>, 13, "靈意解經是相對於字面解經 [literal interpretation] 的一種解經的詮釋方法 . . . 它首先是指著一個信念：經文的意思超越了字面的拘限；其次也指著一種釋經方法，就是要發掘經文的隱藏或更深層的含意." Translation: "Spiritual interpretation is a method of interpreting the Bible that contrasts with literal interpretation . . . it first refers to a belief: the meaning of a passage goes beyond the limits of the literal meaning; second, it refers to an interpretive method that wants to discover a passage's hidden or deeper level of meaning." Unlike 梁 who equates this with allegorical interpretation, Wan argues that spiritual interpretation is focused on "moral cultivation" in "this world," rather than another dimension or world

spiritualization and salvation of the soul, which also yields spiritual knowledge (靈知) and spiritual feeling (靈覺).[76] He relatedly referred to spiritual illumination (*lingguang*, 靈光) of the soul, including the mind, and emphasized the effect that such illumination has on a person's moral discernment and knowledge of God.[77] There seems to be a general correspondence here to what Nee and some Chinese Christians today call *liangguang* (亮光), or spontaneous, suprarational flashes of insight into the meaning of the biblical text.[78] Wan highlights the resemblance between Jia's hermeneutics and neo-Confucian reading of the classics for moral cultivation.[79]

Jia's trichotomous theological anthropology (靈魂體) prioritizing the spirit has similarities to Nee's (though is not necessarily identical).[80] In accordance with Jia's emphasis on the spirit, he called the seminary that he ran for twenty years (1936–56) a "school of spirituality" (靈修學院), rather than a "seminary" (神學院) or otherwise.[81] This recalls the aforementioned challenges to the identity and mission of Chinese seminaries. In any case, if there is an underlying theological anthropology sharply dividing between spirit and soul (cf. Heb 4:12), should seminaries prioritize the spirit or the soul? If both, how? Either way, a seminary that is even perceived as overemphasizing the mind could easily be perceived as unspiritual. In contrast, the integration of faith and learning (i.e., heart and mind) as proposed above serves as a response to the sharp division between spirit and soul/mind.

As we might expect by now, the emphasis on embodied, moral, and practical knowledge has parallels in the Confucian classics themselves. The opening line of the *Analects* (1.1) praises the one who constantly learns and

---

as was common for Western allegorists ("Competing Tensions," 104).

76. Jia, 完全救法, 1:126–27.

77. Jia, 完全救法, 1:123, 127.

78. Regarding Nee's use of this term, see Lam, 屬靈神學, 134.

79. Wan, "Competing Tensions," 104. See also his discussion of Chen Chonggui on 97, 104–7.

80. Jia, 完全救法, 1:14, 123–31, 138–46. Like Nee he uses the temple to explain his trichotomous anthropology. Given Nee's mention of Keswick writers (including Andrew Murray), note the same temple analogy in Murray, *Best from All His Works*, 105–11 (original source: *Spirit of Christ*, 1888). He assigns mind, feeling, and will to the soul (106), which should be ruled by the spirit (109). Cf. Murray, *Best of Andrew Murray*, 95–98 (original source: *Spirit of Christ*), which defines the "flesh" as the fallen soul and body (95) and warns against trusting in the "natural mind" rather than recognizing "the absolute need of the Spirit's personal teaching" (97).

81. Chiu, "Constructing a Model," 47. Like HBI (see above), Jia's seminary should also be assessed in terms of the issues Noll raises.

Integration of Faith, Learning, and Ministry

practices what is learned ("To learn and to practice what is learned repeatedly, is it not pleasant?").[82] Commentators explain that the kind of learning in view here is not so much propositional, abstract, and/or theoretical knowledge but rather self-cultivation/transformation, practical know-how, and embodied abilities.[83] Indeed, when a person is learning how to live, act, and be, anything less falls far short. Correspondingly, Covell draws attention to modern Chinese affinity for experiential knowledge and intuition gained from common sense.[84]

## IDEAS FOR MOVING FORWARD

The preceding discussion has shown that whether we are looking at Chinese evangelicals' implied definitions of "spiritual" and "practical," influential Chinese Christians of previous generations, observations about Chinese culture broadly, and/or Confucian teaching, there is a very strong value placed on experiential, practical learning along with self-cultivation (for Christians, "spiritual life"). While certainly respecting this long-standing tradition, I believe that Chinese seminaries that also value academics play a crucial role for Chinese Christians in creating more space to love the Lord with all our minds in all that entails for academic study and cultural engagement. If seminaries like CWTS have a solid grasp of this, then we will not only serve our students better but also indirectly help create such space in churches through them. Furthermore, through conferences, lectures, and other events that serve broader audiences, we have the chance to articulate directly to churches the importance of Christians truly loving the Lord with all their minds (CUV/RCUV: 盡意).

From another perspective, the close relationship of learning, practice, and personal growth, whether Confucian or Christian, is itself an act of integration. So whereas on the one hand I wish for more careful thinking about implied dichotomies, on the other hand I also want to affirm the integration of learning, practice, and character. Of course, I am further suggesting that the value placed on learning be expanded to include theological and other subjects. The Bible itself is certainly intended to cultivate spiritual life (as understood by Chinese Christians), but it also does more

---

82. Ni, *Understanding the* Analects, 79. Original: 学而时习之，不亦说乎？Cf. Confucius, Analects 1.7; 6.3.

83. Ni, *Understanding the* Analects, 70–73, 79–80; Confucius, Analects, 1.

84. Covell, *Confucius, Buddha, and Christ*, 12.

## Integrating Theology, Church, and Ministry in a Chinese Seminary

(e.g., teaches doctrine and theology, grounds our faith in history, provides a metanarrative for understanding the world). If this is granted, the synthesis of learning and practice must also be adjusted to accommodate subjects that are not obviously related to self-cultivation or are not immediately practical. For Chinese seminaries, we can still place a high value on spiritual formation and character and simultaneously affirm the value of learning theological subjects and others also. Ideally, academics would even be seen as part of a more holistic formation.

As we have seen above, there are both biblical and practical-missional reasons to treat study and intellectual growth as something that should be a regular part of a Christian's life. Again, this does not mean that all should be scholars or theologians, and this would look different for each individual. It could be as simple as reading a book or article that is intellectually challenging, discussing a ministry issue from a theological perspective with another person, starting a teaching series that requires more preparatory study than usual, attending a lecture on a topic of interest, refreshing biblical languages, or continuing education of some kind. Either way, the development of the mind should be more than peripheral or something left for when there is time, as *Analects* 1.6 and 7.6 would suggest.[85] Aforementioned biblical reasons include the Great Commandment (Matt 22:36–40), the call to take every thought captive to Christ (2 Cor 10:5), the need for our minds to be renewed (Rom 12:2), and the relationship between faith and learning (Prov 1:7). To these may be added the reality that Paul both was aware of the spiritual dimension in misunderstandings of the gospel (2 Cor 3:14–15; 4:4) but still used persuasion and cultural engagement in his ministry (e.g., Acts 17:2–4, 16–18, 22–28). Surely if eating and drinking can be done to the glory of God and the good of others (1 Cor 10:31), then so can study and academics.

My hope is that Dockery's call to embrace the "both-ands" of heart and mind, faith and learning, piety and truth, etc., would be taken seriously and ultimately accepted and pursued. Within Chinese circles, I have further suggested a broadening of what is commonly considered "spiritual" and "practical," which is in fact a "both-and" view of spiritual and academic, practical and theoretical/theological. Though certainly not identical, the items in each pair are more intertwined than is sometimes acknowledged. To take a biblical example, we know that Paul often grounds his more "practical" teaching in detailed theological exposition (e.g., Rom

---

85. See Confucius, *Analects*, 3, 65–66; Ni, *Understanding the Analects*, 83–84, 192–94.

## Integration of Faith, Learning, and Ministry

12–16 in relation to the preceding). We also know that handling new "practical" challenges to the church, whether political, societal, or otherwise, on the fly without sufficient theological grounding can be risky. Even though seminary studies cannot possibly prepare students for every unforeseen challenge, the theological training and grounding is still helpful for facing them when they do arise.

For practical and missional purposes, a greater engagement of our minds with biblical and theological subjects, and other subjects for that matter, is an important way in which evangelicals can engage culture and society. When evangelical leaders engage in this way according to both their gifting and present needs, we have the potential to influence those we serve to adopt a similar posture and to engage similarly. The alternative is closing ourselves off to society in this major area. As we know, this would hurt our public witness, hinder the passing down of the faith to the next generation, and worsen the division and polarization that is too common already. The internet and information age that we live in makes such isolation practically impossible anyway. I trust that readers agree that we ought to engage our world as much as possible in wise, biblically faithful ways. González further reminds us that the Reformation, in whose tradition we stand, "began in a university environment, and it was the universities that provided its most important leaders for several generations. Martin Luther, a priest and Augustinian monk, was above all a university professor."[86] Thus, encouraging Christians to develop their minds for the sake of engaging the world with the gospel continues the best of both evangelical and Reformation traditions.

Since I have been fortunate to teach both American and Chinese evangelicals, I would suggest that mutual awareness, dialogue, and even collaboration would likely benefit both sides. It is not that one needs to become like the other or that both should meet in the middle, but rather there are strengths on each side that deserve careful consideration concerning how these strengths might look in another cultural context. Whereas Chinese seminaries have given much attention to spiritual formation, we can benefit from voices and institutions that, while not neglecting spiritual formation either, have given careful thought to a Christian approach to academics and study. For our own sake, we should seek out individuals and institutions in American evangelicalism (and beyond) that have more successfully integrated academics, and even scholarship, with Christian living

---

86. González, *History of Theological Education*, 69.

and ministry. After all, although cultures differ and should be respected, neither side is inherently more spiritual or academically gifted than the other. To guard against unwitting cultural imposition, this will also require consideration of the relationship between academic standards and culture, as well as teaching methods and culture.[87]

## CONCLUSION

The story of famed evangelist John Sung throwing his diplomas and awards into the Pacific Ocean from a boat while on his way back to China from America is one of the best-known incidents in his life.[88] This dramatic action, however, communicates a very negative view of education and learning as being "worldly." Certainly, if such things become an idol, they should be dealt with seriously. On the other hand, Chinese people, including Christians, as a rule highly value education and not necessarily in an idolatrous way. What is the Chinese Christian to do? It is my belief that we need to consider not only present needs and pressures but also biblical teaching, our own cultural history, our specifically Chinese Christian history, our relationship to fundamentalism and evangelicalism more broadly, the nature and history of theological education, current approaches to theological education from outside of our circles, and perhaps even more. Although the preceding has only scratched the surface of these issues, let us continue the conversation and move forward together in more effectively integrating faith, learning, and ministry in Chinese theological education for the glory of God and for the sake of the nations. After all, if John Sung actually saved his doctoral diploma as some versions of the story say, then, metaphorically speaking, perhaps other intellectual pursuits can be redeemed also.[89]

---

87. For select issues that concern teaching and learning in a Chinese context, see Ott, *Teaching and Learning*, 120, 179, 184–88, 266.

88. Ireland, *John Song*, 49–50, helpfully discusses different versions of this story in n53. Accordingly, based on the warning against the scribes in Mark 12:38–40, Sung calls the "mind/brain" (頭腦), which he associates with the "soul" (魂), one of the "chains" (鎖鏈) that must be broken in his sermon "Break Every Chain," in 宋尚節 [Sung], <培靈集> 港三版, 31.

89. Ireland, *John Song*, 41–43, relatedly notes fundamentalist missionaries' and Sung's frequent mention of his PhD in chemistry.

# Integration of Faith, Learning, and Ministry
## BIBLIOGRAPHY

Aikman, David. *Jesus in Beijing: How Christianity Is Transforming China and Changing the Global Balance of Power.* Washington, DC: Regnery, 2006.

Calvin, John. *Institutes of the Christian Religion.* Translated by Henry Beveridge. Grand Rapids: Eerdmans, 1989.

Chiu, Brian Siu Kit. "Constructing a Model of Theological Education for Contemporary China: Retrieving Insights from Jia Yuming." *InSights Journal* 6.2 (2021) 45–59.

Chow, Alexander. *Theosis, Sino-Christian Theology and the Second Chinese Enlightenment: Heaven and Humanity in Unity.* Christianities of the World. New York: Palgrave Macmillan, 2013.

Christian Witness Theological Seminary. "Vision Statement." https://www.cwts.edu/mission/?lang=en.

Confucius. *Confucius* Analects: *With Selection from Traditional Commentaries.* Translated by Edward Slingerland. Indianapolis: Hackett, 2003.

Covell, Ralph R. *Confucius, the Buddha, and Christ: A History of the Gospel in Chinese.* American Society of Missiology Series. Maryknoll, NY: Orbis, 1986.

Dockery, David S. *Renewing Minds: Serving Church and Society through Christian Higher Education.* Nashville: B&H Academic, 2007.

Fulton, Brent. *China's Urban Christians: A Light That Cannot Be Hidden.* Studies in Chinese Christianity. Eugene, OR: Pickwick, 2015.

González, Justo L. *The History of Theological Education.* Nashville: Abingdon, 2015.

Hopkins, Evan Henry. *The Law of Liberty in the Spiritual Life.* London: Marshall Brothers, 1884.

Ireland, Daryl R. *John Song: Modern Chinese Christianity and the Making of a New Man.* Studies in World Christianity. Waco, TX: Baylor University Press, 2020.

Kwok, Wai Luen. "Sola Scriptura's and the Chinese Union Version Bible's Impact upon Conservative Christian Leaders: The Case of Watchman Nee and Wang Mingdao." *Journal of the Royal Asiatic Society* 30.1 (Jan. 2020) 93–103.

Murray, Andrew. *The Best from All His Works.* Edited by Charles Erlandson. Nashville: Nelson, 1988.

———. *The Best of Andrew Murray.* Grand Rapids, MI: Baker, 1991.

Nee, Watchman. *The Normal Christian Life.* Wheaton, IL: Tyndale, 1977.

———. *The Spiritual Man.* Vol. 1. New York: Christian Fellowship Publishers, 1968.

———. *The Spiritual Man.* Vol. 3. New York: Christian Fellowship Publishers, 1968.

Ni, Peimin. *Understanding the* Analects *of Confucius: A New Translation of* Lunyu *with Annotations.* SUNY Series in Chinese Philosophy and Culture. Albany, NY: State University of New York Press, 2017.

Noll, Mark A. "Evangelical Intellectual Life: Reflections on the Past." In *The State of the Evangelical Mind: Reflections on the Past, Prospects for the Future*, edited by Todd C. Ream et al., 26–30. Downers Grove, IL: IVP Academic, 2018.

———. "The Evangelical Mind Today." *First Things*, Oct. 2004. https://www.firstthings.com/article/2004/10/the-evangelical-mind-today.

———. *The Scandal of the Evangelical Mind.* Grand Rapids, MI: Eerdmans, 1995.

Ott, Craig. *Teaching and Learning across Cultures: A Guide to Theory and Practice.* Grand Rapids, MI: Baker Academic, 2021.

Sailhamer, John H. "The Nature, Purpose, and Tasks of a Theological Seminary." In *The Seminary as a Textual Community: Exploring John Sailhamer's Vision for Theological Education*, edited by Ched Spellman and Jason K. Lee, 3–45. Dallas: Fontes, 2021.

Starr, Chloë, ed. *Reading Christian Scriptures in China*. London: T&T Clark, 2008.

Tie, Peter L. H. "Spirit, Scripture, Saints, and Seminary: Toward a Reappropriation of 'Spirit Illumination' in 'Scripture Interpretation' for Seminarians." In *Spirit Wind: The Doctrine of the Holy Spirit in Global Theology—A Chinese Perspective*, edited by Peter L. H. Tie and Justin T. T. Tan, 3–36. Eugene, OR: Pickwick, 2021.

Trueman, Carl R. "The Failure of Evangelical Elites." *First Things*, Nov. 2021. https://www.firstthings.com/article/2021/11/the-failure-of-evangelical-elites.

Tseng, Gloria S. "Revival Preaching and the Indigenization of Christianity in Republican China." *International Bulletin of Missionary Research* 38.4 (Oct. 2014) 177–82.

Wan, Enoch. "Critiquing the Method of Traditional Western Theology and Calling for Sino-Theology." *Global Missiology English* 1.1 (2003). http://ojs.globalmissiology.org/index.php/english/article/view/438.

Wan, Sze-kar. "Competing Tensions: A Search for May Fourth Biblical Hermeneutics." In *Reading Christian Scriptures in China*, edited by Chloë Starr, 97–117. T&T Clark Theology. London: T&T Clark, 2008.

Xiyi Yao, Kevin. "The Hunan Bible Institute (Biola-in-China): A Stronghold of Fundamentalist Bible Training in China, 1916–1952." *Studies in World Christianity* 27.2 (July 2021) 124–44.

Yeh, Allen L. *Polycentric Missiology: Twenty-First Century Mission from Everyone to Everywhere*. Downers Grove, IL: IVP Academic, 2016.

倪柝聲:《讀經之路》.香港:香港教會書室, 1976.

林榮洪 (Lam Wing-Hung):《屬靈神學:倪柝聲思想的研究》.香港:中國神學研究院, 1985.

賈玉銘 (Jia Yuming).《完全救法》.共二卷.臺北縣:基督徒天恩社, 1966.

王明道 (Wang Mingdao):"怎样读圣经?"《靈食季刊》6 (1928) 59–67.

宋尚節:「斷開一切的鎖鏈」,《培靈集》.香港:晨星書屋, 1975, 三版.

梁家麟, <為靈意解經辯誣>,《教牧期刊》3 (1997): 11–47.

# Truth, Being True, and Theological Education

ESTHER NG

## INTRODUCTION

WE LIVE IN A time when it is often difficult to distinguish between truth and falsehood, or between right and wrong. Thus we encounter imitation merchandise and counterfeit money; lies or half-truths spoken by politicians and journalists; hoaxes in emails, text messages, and social media; distortions in historical accounts, in reports of scientific research, and even in presentations of religious convictions. Under such circumstances, how should Christians live? The purpose of this article is to explore and clarify the underlying issues, focusing on matters of truth in relation to epistemology, facticity, authenticity, and sincerity. In each section, we will first give an account of biblical teaching, then discuss current challenges, followed by outlining the responses that Christians can have to these challenges. Finally, I will offer some tentative suggestions on how theological education and local churches can cooperate in the face of such challenges, with the hope of generating further discussion and inviting fresh ideas from readers.

Integrating Theology, Church, and Ministry in a Chinese Seminary

## DEFINITION OF TERMS

Whether it is the Hebrew word אֱמֶת (*emeth*), the Greek word ἀλήθεια (*alētheia*), or the English word *truth*, as well as their derivatives, each of them can have several connotations.[1] This is less so in Chinese, however, since for compound terms beginning with the adjective *zhen* (真, real, true), each has more specific connotations. In any case, to preclude misunderstanding and unnecessary disputes, I will first clarify my use of the two nouns *zhen li* (真理) and *zhen xiang* (真相) and the two adjectives *zhen shi* (真實) and *zhen cheng* (真誠).

1. *zhen li* (真理): universal and eternal truths concerning objective reality and their underlying principles.

2. *zhen xiang* (真相): the facts and true state of affairs of historical events and current situations (including scientific discoveries and developments).

3. *zhen shi* (真實): corresponding to objective reality; not illusory, fake, counterfeit, or fabricated.

4. *zhen cheng* (真誠): consistency of a person's demeanor and words with his or her inward being; honest, earnest, not hypocritical; with further connotations of being reliable, faithful, not fickle.

## *ZHEN LI* (TRUTH, 真理) AND *ZHEN SHI* (REAL, 真實)

### A. Biblical Teaching[2]

According to Scripture, objective immutable truth (ἀλήθεια, *alētheia*) exists in the world and can be comprehended by human beings and expressed in words. For example, through observing the natural world, humans should be able to deduce the existence of a Creator, as well as his power and attributes (Rom 1:20; cf. Acts 14:16–17). But human beings oftentimes suppress this truth (Rom 1:18–20).

As for the divine Son, Jesus Christ, he not only bore witness to the truth and communicated truth (John 1:17; 8:40; 18:37), but also claimed to be "the way, and the truth, and the life" (John 14:6). The apostle John

---

1. See Palmer, "Truth," 1213; Ritzema, "Truth."
2. Unless otherwise specified, biblical passages are hereafter cited from the NIV.

also testified that "the Word became flesh and made his dwelling among us. We have seen his glory, the glory of the one and only Son, who came from the Father, full of grace and truth" (John 1:14). Likewise the apostle Paul claimed that "truth is in Jesus Christ" (Eph 4:21). Jesus further promised that whoever obeys his word (his disciples) will know the truth and thereby be set free (John 8:31–32).

With regard to the Holy Spirit (the Advocate, παράκλητος, *parakletos*), Jesus called him the Spirit of Truth (John 14:17; 15:26; 16:13). As the triune God is the source and embodiment of truth, God's words and actions inevitably pertain to truth: God uses the word of truth to give new life to believers (Jas 1:18) and set them free (John 8:31–32); his word is the truth that sanctifies believers (John 17:17); the Holy Spirit will guide the apostles into all the truth (John 16:13). It is noteworthy that the New Testament often refers to the good news of Jesus's substitutionary death as the truth (e.g., Gal 2:14; Eph 1:13; Col 1:5; 2 Thess 2:13–14; 2 Tim 2:15; 1 Pet 1:12, 22) that is applicable to all mankind (John 3:16; 1 Tim 2:4–6; 1 John 2:2). As the church of God proclaims the gospel, it is thus described as the pillar and foundation of truth (1 Tim 3:15). Since Paul sought to defend the truth of the cross, he willingly endured persecution (Gal 4:16; 5:11; 6:12) and risked his life as a herald of the gospel (1 Tim 2:7). Furthermore, since truth is more than mental concepts but should lead to a godly life (Titus 1:1), believers should obey the truth and live accordingly (Gal 5:7; 3 John 3–4).

Here we should also mention that, according to the Gospel of John, Jesus is the true light (1:9), the true bread (6:32), and the true vine (15:1); the Father is the only true God (17:3). The letter to the Hebrews describes Jesus as ministering in the true sanctuary (Heb 8:2; 9:24). The epithet "true" (ἀληθινός *alēthinos*) in these passages is primarily used in contrast to the prior imperfect or counterfeit copies. In view of the true nature of Jesus's being and work, those who worship the Father must worship him in spirit and in truth (*alētheia*, John 4:23).[3]

---

3. Commentators interpret the phrase ἐν πνεύματι καὶ ἀληθείᾳ (*en pneumati kai alētheia[i]*) in various ways, e.g., understanding the "spirit" (*pneuma*) to refer to the Holy Spirit (as in the NIV, New Chinese Version) or the human spirit, and translating the word *alētheia* as "truth," or "sincerity" (Chinese Union Version). A possible translation of the phrase is "in spirit authentically."

## B. Challenges to Biblical Teaching and Possible Christian Responses

### 1. Modernism in Philosophy[4]

From the time of the Enlightenment to the middle of the twentieth century, though Western societies generally accepted the existence of universal objective truths, the intelligentsia usually have disdained treating God's special revelation (Christ, the Bible) as the foundation of truth. Rather, they exalt human reason as the ultimate objective standard to judge claims of truth, above church authority or biblical teaching. Known as "modernism," this stream of thought is still influential in the West and may even be the mainstream among Chinese scholars today.

In response to this stream of thinking and in line with biblical teaching, we should point out the limitations and inadequacy of human reason while consenting to the importance of reason. As created beings, humans have limited knowledge (cf. Job 38–39). Not only do human beings have limited knowledge of revelation in nature, but we also have limited knowledge of God's special revelation in Scripture owing to our distance in time and space from the original recipients of this revelation. With our limited knowledge, it is puerile for humans to cast doubt on the existence of God or to critique the Bible, like "mayflies trying to shake a huge tree" (i.e., overreaching and futile).

Moreover, besides being created beings, humans rebel against God and are by nature sinners such that their reason has been distorted. Paul describes the situation well: "although they knew God, they neither glorified him as God nor gave thanks to him, but their thinking became futile and their foolish hearts were darkened" (Rom 1:21–22). As a result, humans inevitably make idols and worship them foolishly. Paul further tells us that the minds of unbelievers are blinded by Satan "so that they cannot see the light of the gospel that displays the glory of Christ, who is the image of God" (2 Cor 4:4; cf. John 8:44). Moreover, false teachers not only are themselves deceived; they also deceive others (2 Tim 3:13).

These biblical passages clearly show that human reason cannot be a neutral final arbiter of truth; human logic and presuppositions may very

---

4. See Leffel, "Our Old Challenge," 19–30. For a succinct description in Chinese, see Kwan, "From Modernism to Postmodernism," 2–16. Both books discuss the challenges of postmodernism to the Christian faith and include the differences between modernism and postmodernism.

well be false. The following story may serve as an apt illustration: A mentally deluded person thought that he had died. To help him come to his senses and with his permission on the mutually agreed premise that dead persons don't bleed, his doctor used a needle to prick his finger.[5] When the patient discovered that he actually bled, he quickly changed his presupposition and exclaimed, "Dead persons bleed after all!" Likewise, as human beings sin, their minds are darkened, their vision is blinded, and their rational faculty has been distorted.

## 2. Postmodernism in Philosophy[6]

In the second half of the twentieth century, as a result of reflections on and critiques of human reason, postmodernism began to permeate Western societies and areas under their influence. It is asserted that reason is not a neutral universal arbiter of truth, and human beings actually do not have a transcendent position to judge what constitutes absolute truth. Rather, each community has its particular perspective, its own view of things and its own story. In other words, so-called truth is a social construct, a product of history and culture: there are only partial truths established under specific conditions in the world, and people have no basis to judge which account is more "true." Consequently, postmodern philosophy is characterized by relativism, deconstructionism, antifoundationalism, and even subjectivism. Frequently the analogy of the blind men is employed to buttress the claims of relativism: just as the blind men could only touch and describe different parts of an elephant and so arrived at different understandings of the animal, likewise human beings can only access and describe partial and incomplete truths. Furthermore, some postmodern philosophers often view those who claim to possess absolute truth as people in power who suppress dissidents in the name of truth in order to maintain the status quo. Since so-called truth has become a tool of injustice, people should deconstruct it and expose its social origin.[7]

---

5. I first heard this illustration during a course taught by Dr. John Warwick Montgomery at Trinity Evangelical Divinity School in the 1970s. It has left an indelible impression on my memory.

6. Besides Kwan and Cheung, *Postmodernism and Christianity*, see also Dockery, *Challenge of Postmodernism*; Erickson, *Truth or Consequences*.

7. See the summary in Neuhaus, "Is There Life after Truth?," 23–38. For the view of Michel Foucault, see Kwan, "Challenge of Foucault's View," 135–61 (English abstract on 160–61). On a discussion on Foucault, Derrida, and Rorty, see Erickson, *Truth or*

## Integrating Theology, Church, and Ministry in a Chinese Seminary

With the influx of postmodernism, some Christian scholars welcome it as a positive development, seeing that it demotes or reduces the hubris of rationalism and also provides the basis and opportunity for Christians to claim their voice in public discourse.[8] In response, we may agree that there is certainly a relative dimension to the truths and facts that humans know. First, owing to the progressive nature of divine revelation and the arrival of a new era with Christ's first coming, regulations on sacrifices, festivals, and foods in the Old Testament only have symbolic or typological significance in the New Testament, and Christians (especially non-Jews) are not obligated to observe them literally (Col 2:16–23; Heb 8–10).

Second and related to the first observation, Paul instructs believers to be firm in their own minds concerning the observance of special days and food regulations but to be open to different views and practices and not to dispute over them (Rom 14–15). In other words, Paul did not compromise over certain truths, but urged Christians to accommodate other believers in matters of secondary importance (cf. 1 Cor 9:19–23).[9]

Furthermore, in the light of apostolic teaching in the New Testament and our own experience, we can be certain that there is, and should be, room for improvement in our individual and collective Christian understanding and appropriation of truth (see, for example, Eph 4:11–13; Phil 1:9; 2 Pet 1:6–8). Until the return of Christ, our knowledge is always limited, and "we see only a reflection as in a mirror" (1 Cor 13:12). In contrast to the eventual cessation of prophecy, tongues-speaking, and knowledge, love endures forever (1 Cor 13:8–13); no wonder love is the most excellent way!

Christians' understanding of truth is imperfect and we may find partial truths in other religions or philosophical systems. Indeed, of the list of things that Paul urges believers to think about, first and foremost is "whatever is true [ἀληθῆ, $al\bar{e}th\bar{e}$]" (Phil 4:8). Nevertheless, in view of the biblical teaching mentioned earlier, as Christians, we should not wholeheartedly embrace postmodernism. Rather, we should maintain that absolute truth does exist and that statements on truth can be evaluated according to their merits and relative correspondence to truth.[10] Furthermore, as responsible

---

*Consequences*, 231–32, 249.

8. See, for example, Grenz, *Primer on Postmodernism*.

9. Here we may benefit from the dictum attributed to Augustine: "In essentials, unity; in non-essentials, liberty; in all things, charity." See Kwan and Cheung, *Postmodernism and Christianity*, 365.

10. This is the position of Critical Realism; Kwan and Cheung, *Postmodernism and Christianity*, 159, 163, 203; Erickson, *Truth or Consequences*, 257–67. See also Kai-man

## Truth, Being True, and Theological Education

citizens, we should engage in conversation with people of different religions and convictions. In addition, while postmodernism claims that "there is no absolute truth," its proponents actually treat this assertion as absolute truth. Thus this assertion is self-defeating and untenable.[11]

As for the analogy of the blind men, it too is inadequate: unless there are people with normal vision on the scene, there is no way to tell whether the blind men are actually in touch with the same object. Similarly, when a person claims that all religions and such discourses are referring to the same thing, or denies that humans can know the truth, he or she is already presupposing a transcendent point of reference or view.[12]

If one asserts that claims of truth are to be deconstructed and their social origins revealed, why is it that claims in the name of "justice" and formulations of "social origin" may not be deconstructed themselves as well?[13] Moreover, if the postmodernist deconstruction of truth were to be consistently applied, and people holding different views and positions cannot communicate with one another and discuss on the common basis of reason, what means is available for one position to win people's hearts and become public policy other than by shouting louder to drown out opposing views, stirring up people's emotions, and even resorting to violence? In fact, advocates of tolerance and diversity are frequently the most intolerant of those who claim that absolute truths exist![14]

### 3. Identity Politics[15]

It is difficult for pure and consistent postmodernism to provide meaning and direction to life. No wonder in many places far more prevalent are views on truth and various political movements based on identities such as social status, nationality, race, sex, sexual orientation, gender, etc. Extremists in

---

Kwan's criteria on evaluating worldviews in his Chinese book *Twelve Lectures on the Christian Worldview*, 286–88.

11. See Erickson, *Truth or Consequences*, 204–5.

12. Keller, "Reason for God," 62–63, citing Michael Polanyi and Lesslie Newbigin in a rebuttal of the argument.

13. Erickson, *Truth or Consequences*, 205–6.

14. Carson, *Intolerance of Tolerance*; MacDonald, *Diversity Illusion*.

15 For seeing identity politics as the predominant thinking subsequent to Postmodernism, see Williams, *Confronting Injustice*, 117, 153 (described by Williams as Post-Postmodernism, but this term has other connotations and is not adopted here); Murray, *Madness of Crowds*, 1–2.

## Integrating Theology, Church, and Ministry in a Chinese Seminary

political movements arising from such identities tend to attribute false consciousness to privileged or dominating groups, such as the upper classes, people of wealth, whites, males, heterosexuals, and cis-gendered. These are said to harbor implicit bias against others and a tendency to lord over others, whereas minorities and marginalized groups (e.g. the poor, colored, female, LGBTQ[16]) are able to see matters with true discernment and thus possess truth. Since justice and history are on the side of the minorities, people should fight for justice, eradicate old evils, including the reform of thought, and even participate in a revolution to usher in a new society and a new era.[17]

To many Christians, it seems biblical to sympathize with marginalized groups who are discriminated against and to fight for justice and equity. However, those who think that marginalized and minority people inevitably possess truth and not false consciousness tend to deify them and demonize the majority groups, ignoring the sinful nature of all human beings and the possibility of distorted consciousness and misdirected hatred that may afflict those previously hurt by interpersonal relationships.[18] It is also easy to forget that other groups are equally human beings created in the image of God and bearers of dignity. Attempts to brainwash, vilify, coerce, and oppress the majority groups are likewise unbiblical. Christians should be cautious and not cause harm by ill-informed good intentions.[19]

---

16. LGBTQ is the acronym for lesbian, gay, bisexual, transgender, and queer/questioning.

17. People under the broad umbrella of LGBTQ have various identities, and those claiming one identity do not necessarily belong to, or agree with, the political movement of that particular identity. Furthermore, an activist in one particular political movement may disagree with the political movement of another identity. For example, the feminist author Sheila Jeffreys describes how the transgender movement is inimical to feminism and hurts lesbians; see her *Gender Hurts*. Nevertheless, activists for "social justice" stress the intersectionality of identities and the hierarchy of oppression such that any disparaging remark or action against the "minorities" (especially those most oppressed) would come under their ferocious attack. It is no wonder that the self-professed gay writer Douglas Murray castigates the extreme behavior of advocates of the gay movement, radical feminism, racial justice movement, and transgender movement; see his *Madness of Crowds*.

18. For a good analysis, see Williams, *Confronting Injustice*, 139–48. Critiques of Marxist social analysis are also applicable to other political movements based on identity; see, e.g., Kai-man Kwan in Kwan and Cheung, *Post-Modernist Culture and Christianity*, 155 ("Postmodern Thought and Christian Theology"). For an analysis and critique of political ideologies in general, see also Koyzis, *Political Visions and Illusions*.

19. Williams, *Confronting Injustice*, 162–66; Chen, "Crisis of the Foundation," 8–11 (Chinese).

# Truth, Being True, and Theological Education
## *ZHEN XIANG* (真相, FACTS), *ZHEN SHI* (真實, TRUE) AND *ZHEN CHENG* (真誠, BEING TRUE)

### A. Biblical Teaching

Though Chinese Bible translations do not generally use the term *zhen xiang*, still in some contexts, the Old Testament word אֱמֶת (*emeth*) and the New Testament word ἀλήθεια (*alētheia*) as well as their derivatives do have the connotation of *zhen xiang* (facts or state of affairs). For example, when charges were made in ancient Israelite society, the judge should investigate the case, find out the facts on the basis of testimony and evidence, and then come to a verdict (Deut 13:14; 17:4; 22:20). After the Queen of Sheba visited Solomon in person, she found out that the rumors about him were true, in accordance with the facts (1 Kgs 10:6–7). In the New Testament, persons who spoke the truth (facts) include the woman healed of a hemorrhage (Mark 5:33), the Samaritan woman (John 4:17–18), Jesus (John 16:7), and Paul (Acts 26:25; 2 Cor 12:6; 1 Tim 2:7). These examples show clearly that facts can be ascertained and described. However, other biblical passages indicate that we don't necessarily know the whole truth of matters this side of heaven. Apart from willful deceit of others, humans are limited in their self-knowledge and may even be self-deceived for years (Jas 1:22; 1 John 1:8). Accordingly, Paul advised Timothy to be extremely careful when dealing with charges against elders (1 Tim 5:19–22, 24–25). Likewise, our Lord Jesus teaches us to judge people's character not merely by their words but also by their deeds (fruit) (Matt 7:15–23). At the end of the day, we can only find out all the facts when the Lord returns to judge mankind and give the ultimate verdict (1 Cor 3:13–15; 4:1–15).

In any case, whether people's words correspond to the facts is a good indicator of their character and trustworthiness. This is why, after he became the vizier of Egypt, Joseph kept one of his brothers in custody and commanded the rest to bring along their youngest brother to test whether they spoke the truth or were actually spies (Gen 42:16). Along the same vein, whether a prophecy was fulfilled in real life was a criterion to judge between true and false prophets (Deut 18:22; 1 Kgs 17:24).

Since words reflect what is in the heart, a person who constantly speaks truthful (*zhen shi*) words is a genuine, faithful, and trustworthy (*zhen cheng*) person. As God is by nature true and faithful (Exod 34:6; Deut 32:4; Pss 89:14; 108:2), he is faithful in his dealings with his people Israel (Neh 9:33; Ps 111:7–8; Hos 2:19–20; Mic 7:20), individual righteous

Integrating Theology, Church, and Ministry in a Chinese Seminary

persons (Gen 24:27; 32:9–10; Ps 119:151) such as David and the Messiah (Pss 61:7; 132:11), and all people on earth (Ps 96:12–13; Rom 3:4, 7–8). God also requires his elect to be inwardly truthful (Pss 15:1–2; 51:6), speak the truth, and not lie like the devil (Exod 20:16; Deut 5:20; Prov 6:16, 17, 19; Zech 8:16; Matt 5:37; John 8:44; Eph 4:25; 5:9). They are to appoint truthful people as leaders (Exod 18:21; Neh 7:2). God also warns that those who love to lie and practice falsehood will ultimately be excluded from the New Jerusalem (Rev 21:8, 27; 22:15).

## B. Challenges to Biblical Teaching and Possible Christian Responses

Doubtlessly the Bible teaches us to speak the truth and be truthful. Nevertheless, from ancient times to now there have been people who distort the truth and manipulate the masses such that people generally are afraid and dare not be truthful or tell the truth.

### 1. *Distorting the Truth in History and in Stories*

It is said that during the reign of the second emperor of the Qin Dynasty in China, his prime minister Zhao Gao pointed to a deer and called it a horse so as to test the loyalty of the court officials to himself. In fear of his overbearing power and threats, all the officials agreed that the animal before them was a horse and not a deer. This caused the emperor to be mentally confused and he was soon afterward forced to die by Zhao's servants. This is the story behind the Chinese idiom "calling a deer a horse," which is still used today to depict distortions of the truth. We may call this the "hard-sell" version of truth distortion. In the West, George Orwell's novel *1984* portrays how the Ministry of Truth in a totalitarian country twists facts and obscures truth using coercion. Meanwhile we find a description of a "soft-sell" version of distortion in Hans Christian Andersen's story of "The Emperor's New Clothes" that vividly portrays people's blind worship of intelligence and wisdom. Just because the charlatan tailors alleged that only the wise could see the new clothes they made for the emperor, the emperor himself, all his officials, and denizens in his kingdom pretended to be wise and agreed that he wore new clothes. Eventually it took a child to shatter the falsehood and tell the truth that the emperor didn't wear any clothes at all. Another fairy tale in the West that includes a soft-sell version of truth distortion is found in Lewis Carroll's *Alice in Wonderland: Through the Looking Glass*. Here Humpty Dumpty tells Alice that, except for proper names, he is able to alter the usual meaning of any word to give it a novel twist to suit his fancy.

## 2. Contemporary Versions of Distortions of Truth (Facts)

On the surface, the four stories mentioned above seem irrelevant to our twenty-first century. Yet if we pay closer attention we will discover that contemporary fake news and distortions of truth, whether in their soft-sell or hard-sell varieties, are actually current versions of "calling the deer a horse," the Ministry of Truth, "The Emperor's New Clothes," and Humpty Dumpty. For instance, in order to ensure so-called national security or retain their positions, government officials at various levels of dictatorial regimes often withhold factual information from the public and suppress dissidents with an iron fist and harsh treatment, thereby forcing the masses to "call the deer a horse" and utter false statements sometimes against their conscience. Meanwhile their leaders claim that the nation upholds multi-party rule and its people enjoy freedom and democracy.[20] As for the United States and so-called democratic free societies in the West, distortions of truth likewise exist in word and deed. For the past two decades, they generally occur in soft-sell versions to achieve "politically correct" goals.[21] For instance, for college admission and employee hiring, it is often claimed that diversity in background and an equal proportion of females to males are more desirable than academic performance and professional excellence. However, with the proliferation of identity politics, not only are terms such as "social justice" and "equity" given meanings different from traditional understandings, those who wish to change the status quo and fight for an ideal society sometimes even claim that facts don't matter, and it is legitimate to tell half-truths or even spread falsehood.[22] For example, in order to demonstrate the prevalence of systemic racism in the United States, the actual number of

---

20. For historical accounts, see, for example, Solzhenitsyn, *Gulag Archipelago*; Wu, *Chinese Gulag*.

21. This tendency in Western societies is described by Rod Dreher as "soft totalitarianism"; see his *Live Not by Lies*. He points out astutely that this form of totalitarianism is the result of identity politics. Meanwhile, the news commentator Mark Levin calls this tendency and certain developments in the Democratic party American Marxism; see his *American Marxism*.

22. Williams, *Confronting Injustice*, 137, 162–81; MacDonald, *Diversity Illusion*, 35.

Blacks killed by White policemen is often exaggerated, and any disparity between White and Black Americans is attributed to racial discrimination.[23] In order to showcase the extent of physical violence done by men toward women, the number of women raped by men is often exaggerated.[24] To support the argument that homosexuality is inborn, its prevalence in the general population is often exaggerated (alleged to be 10 percent), and any possible harm caused by homosexual activities to those habitually engaged in them and to society in general is downplayed.[25] For the sake of "equity" to the transgendered, the health risks of sex reassignment surgery are minimized, and males claiming to be transgendered women can freely access women's bathrooms and women's sports.[26] Sometimes activists (e.g., those within the LGBTQ community) relentlessly sue those who oppose their agenda.[27] Radical activists may even resort to brute force (e.g., the riots associated with the Black Lives Matter movement in the summer of 2020).[28] Meanwhile the media and social media (e.g., Facebook, Twitter, YouTube) join in by either completely ignoring the facts unfavorable to their narrative or canceling the comments and accounts of their opponents. After

---

23. Other examples include rewriting Black American history, downplaying the role of Whites who participated in the anti-slavery movement, and ignoring the much higher proportion of Blacks killed at the hands of Blacks in recent decades. See Sowell, *Discrimination and Disparities*; Riley, *Please Stop Helping Us*.

24. See Sommers, *Who Stole Feminism?*, 209–26; MacDonald, *Diversity Illusion*, 117, 124, 137.

25. For the 10 percent figure, see Jones and Yarhouse, *Homosexuality*, 21–46. For a succinct summary of studies on homosexuality, see Jones, "Same-Sex Science," 27–33. For an objective report on findings regarding both homosexuality and transgenderism, see Mayer and McHugh, "Sexuality and Gender Findings," 4–143. For a good discussion in Chinese, see Kwan, *Comment on LGBT Movement*.

26. Jeffreys, *Gender Hurts*; Sprinkle, *Embodied*.

27. Because of Christian convictions, the florist Barronelle Stutzman declined her long-time customer's request to make a floral arrangement at his gay wedding. Likewise the baker Jack Phillips refused to make a special cake for a customer's gay wedding. Both were prosecuted for discrimination in their respective states. Both cases reached the Supreme Court. While Phillips won this case, he was soon prosecuted by the state again, this time for refusing service to celebrate a gender change. The Supreme Court eventually refused to hear Stutzman's case and she had to pay for damages.

28. In the nation-wide protest subsequent to the death of George Floyd while he was under arrest by a White policeman, mobs under the aegis of the Black Lives Matter movement destroyed and looted shops, damaged public buildings, attacked innocent people, and occupied public spaces until the National Guard was called in.

Democrats assumed power at the beginning of 2021, there have been cases of alleged mistreatment and even wrongful imprisonment of dissenters.[29]

## 3. Possible Christian Responses

Whether in totalitarian countries or in so-called democratic free nations in the West, we Christians live in societies that have little regard for the actual facts as long as the end justifies the means. However, our ultimate loyalty belongs to the only true God and his revelation, not to a certain ideology, race, political party, or nation state. We think it is necessary as far as possible to ascertain the facts and speak the truth; we disapprove of attempts to rewrite history or distort findings in science to support a particular narrative. To be sure, as Christians we should love individuals within different groups, but we should also examine political movements with care and discernment. At times, our position may be firm, based on biblical teaching and incontrovertible findings. Thus we may be sure that the LGBTQ movement is generally destructive to the marriage and family structure ordained by God, is harmful to individuals enmeshed in it, and is subversive of social institutions. Likewise, we can be certain that while Critical Race Theory draws attention to the suffering of Blacks in history, its accusations are overblown, its tactics are extreme, and it is in general socially divisive. Both movements are contrary to biblical teaching, and it behooves church leaders to pay attention themselves and to explain to their members what is at stake.

However, it may be difficult to find the truth with regard to certain controversial matters that affect our daily lives. For instance, on the one hand, the heads of nations in the West view global warming (or climate change) as a serious threat to human survival with carbon dioxide emission being the culprit such that the use of fossil fuels should be eventually banned at all costs. But on the other hand, some scientists and even former advocates of environmental protection dissent from this view after years of study on this issue.[30] During the COVID-19 pandemic, numerous medical experts advocated mandatory vaccinations and masks for all (including

---

29. It is alleged that those arrested for breaking into Capitol Hill on January 6, 2021, were mistreated and imprisoned without due process for months. See Kimball, "January 6 Insurrection Hoax."

30. For opposition to green policies, see Epstein, *Moral Case for Fossil Fuels*; Shellenberger, *Apocalypse Never*; Koonin, *Unsettled*. See also http://www.cornwallalliance.org.

children), but other likewise qualified experts opposed this policy for medical and legal reasons.[31] On these two major issues, it seems unwise to toe the official line unquestioningly and dogmatically without checking what the other side is actually saying. For the time being, one may have to live with ambiguity and uncertainty concerning these issues.[32]

In any case, Christians should be truthful themselves and speak the truth, since this is God's will for us and reflects both his nature and the regenerated life of believers. Moreover, telling the truth is conducive to human flourishing and a healthy society.[33] Finally, whatever we say in our lives will be revealed during God's final judgment when the truth of all matters will be manifested (Matt 7:21–23; 12:36–37).

## EVANGELICAL THEOLOGICAL EDUCATION AND THE ROLE OF THE CHURCH

The mission of evangelical seminaries has always been serving local churches and Christian organizations to help them develop pastors, coworkers, and lay leaders who are fit for God's use and who can respond to the challenges of the times. In the contemporary context where truth is suppressed and facts uncertain, it is even more imperative for seminaries to cooperate with local churches and Christian organizations on the basis

---

31. For instance, in 2020 and 2021 thousands of medical doctors and scientists signed declarations to oppose the vaccination of children against COVID-19 and to recommend "natural immunity" for most people as a better policy to control the spread of the pandemic while vaccinating high-risk people and providing medication for patients early in their infection. See https://gbdeclaration.org; https://doctorsandscientistsdeclaration.org.

32. In both Chinese churches and churches of other ethnicities, clergy and lay Christians often discourage and even prohibit the discussion of political issues in church, citing the principle of "separation of church and state" and fearing church schism in the face of diverse political positions. However, we should fully grasp the biblical teaching on truth, the real meaning of "separation of church and state," and learn from church history to avoid repeating past mistakes. For writings in Chinese, see Kwan and Choi, *Christianity and the Debates*, especially 39–44; Louie and Sun, *Call to Political Engagement*, especially 163–73, 175–91. For a good treatment in English, see Grudem, *Politics according to the Bible*, 68–75, 99–103.

33. This is not to say that Christians should tell all the facts they truly know under all circumstances. In totalitarian countries, it is unfortunately true that telling the truth sometimes endangers the life of oneself and of others. In such situations, Christians should of course be as shrewd as serpents. But certainly there must be a bottom line: Christians cannot deny Christ to save one's life.

of shared convictions and common goals to ensure that the gospel truth is transmitted unchanged and unadulterated by secular ways of thinking.

Yet seminaries, local churches and Christian organizations should play different roles in God's universal church. On the one hand, seminary professors usually attend to broader trends in theological studies or delve into certain relevant issues in their specialties such that, to a certain extent, seminaries may serve as a think-tank for local churches and Christian organizations. In addition, evangelical seminaries generally maintain the objectivity of truth (especially the gospel truth) as well as biblical inerrancy and authority. Meanwhile, in their teaching of hermeneutics and other subjects, evangelical professors may instill in students the distinction between non-negotiable truths and interpretations/theories with different degrees of credibility. Thus evangelical seminaries may serve as a protective shield for local churches and Christian organizations. On the other hand, local churches and Christian organizations serve on the front line and have more contact with church members, seekers, and non-Christians. Therefore, seminaries need their input, including their private conversation with seminary professors, open sharing before faculty and students, supervising seminary students in field education, offering financial and prayer support, etc. Only then can theological educators move out of an ivory tower functioning behind closed doors and nurture workers meeting the real needs of contemporary society.

Though the times are changing rapidly and Christians live under more and more difficult circumstances, God's requirement for his servants is constant—being true and truthful. Moreover, as online teaching becomes more prevalent and counterfeiting becomes more widespread, being true and truthful is even more precious. Consequently, a healthy theological education must emphasize spiritual formation and character building in seminary students.

## CONCLUSION

Long, long, ago, Pilate asked contemptuously, "What is truth?" Today all over the world, it seems as if truth is hard to know, facts are hard to ascertain, and true and truthful persons are hard to find. Still, from then till now, Christians are meant to be counter-cultural and serve as the salt and light of the world. May churches, Christian organizations, and seminaries all over the world unite and work alongside one another in their respective roles.

# Integrating Theology, Church, and Ministry in a Chinese Seminary

May we seek the truth, live the truth, and point others to the source of truth and reality—the true, triune God![34]

## BIBLIOGRAPHY

Carson, D. A. *The Intolerance of Tolerance*. Grand Rapids, MI: Eerdmans, 2012. (中譯：卡森《寬容不寬容》, 北京：團結出版社, 2012.)

Chen, Liang-Shwu. "Crisis of the Foundation of American Culture." *Blessings* 22 (Apr. 2021) 8–11. (劉良淑,「美國文化根基的危機」,《恩福》雜誌 (2021年四月) 8–11.)

Dockery, David S. *The Challenge of Postmodernism: An Evangelical Engagement*. 2nd ed. Grand Rapids, MI: Baker Academic, 2001.

Dreher, Rod. *Live Not by Lies: A Manual for Christian Dissidents*. New York: Penguin Random House, 2020.

Epstein, Alex. *The Moral Case for Fossil Fuels*. New York: Penguin, 2014.

Erickson, Millard J. *Truth or Consequences: The Promise and Perils of Postmodernism*. Downers Grove, IL: InterVarsity, 2001.

Grenz, Stanley J. *A Primer on Postmodernism*. Grand Rapids, MI: Eerdmans, 1996.

Grudem, Wayne A. *Politics according to the Bible: A Comprehensive Resource for Understanding Modern Political Issues in Light of Scripture*. Grand Rapids, MI: Zondervan, 2010.

Jeffreys, Sheila. *Gender Hurts: A Feminist Analysis of the Politics of Transgenderism*. New York: Routledge, 2014.

Jones, Stanton L. "Same-Sex Science." *First Things* (Feb. 2012) 27–33.

Jones, Stanton L., and Mark A. Yarhouse. *Homosexuality: The Use of Scientific Research in the Church's Moral Debate*. Downers Grove, IL: InterVarsity, 2000.

Keller, Timothy J. "Reason for God: The Exclusivity of Truth." In *A Place for Truth: Leading Thinkers Explore Life's Hardest Questions*, edited by Dallas Willard, 55–71. Downers Grove, IL: InterVarsity, 2010.

Kimball, Roger. "The January 6 Insurrection Hoax." *Imprimis* (blog), Oct. 1, 2021. https://imprimis.hillsdale.edu/january-6-insurrection-hoax/.

Koonin, Steven E. *Unsettled: What Climate Science Tells Us, What It Doesn't, and Why It Matters*. Dallas: BenBella Books, 2021.

Koyzis, David T. *Political Visions and Illusions: A Survey and Christian Critique of Contemporary Ideologies*. 2nd ed. Downers Grove, IL: IVP Academic, 2019.

Kwan, Kai-man. "The Challenge of Foucault's View on Power/Truth to Christianity: A Preliminary Response." *China Graduate School of Theology Journal* 30 (Jan. 2001) 135–61.

―――. "From Modernism to Postmodernism: A Survey." In *Postmodernism and Christianity*, edited by Kai-man Kwan and Kwok-tung Cheung, 2–16. Hong Kong: Fellowship of Evangelical Students, 2002.

Kwan, Kai-man, and Kwok-tung Cheung, eds. *Postmodernism and Christianity*. Hong Kong: Fellowship of Evangelical Students, 2002. (關啟文、張國棟編,《後現代文化與基督教》香港：學生福音團契, 2002.)

---

34. It is worth mentioning that in his book *Live Not by Lies*, Rod Dreher not only describes the symptoms of "soft totalitarianism" in the United States, he also recounts the lessons to be learned from Christians who lived under hard totalitarianism.

Leffel, Jim. "Our Old Challenge: Modernism." In *The Death of Truth*, edited by Dennis McCallum, 19–30. Minneapolis: Bethany House, 1996.

Levin, Mark R. *American Marxism*. New York: Threshold Editions, 2021.

MacDonald, Heather. *The Diversity Delusion: How Race and Gender Pandering Corrupt the University and Undermine Our Culture*. New York: St. Martin's, 2018.

Mayer, Lawrence S., and Paul R. McHugh. "Sexuality and Gender: Findings from the Biological, Psychological, and Social Sciences." *New Atlantis* 50 (2016) 1–143.

Murray, Douglas. *The Madness of Crowds: Gender, Race and Identity*. London: Bloomsbury, 2019.

Neuhaus, Richard John. "Is There Life after Truth?" In *A Place for Truth: Leading Thinkers Explore Life's Hardest Questions*, edited by Dallas Willard, 23–38. Downers Grove, IL: InterVarsity, 2010.

Palmer, F. H. "Truth." In *New Bible Dictionary*, edited by D. R. W. Wood and I. Howard Marshall, 1213. Downers Grove, IL: InterVarsity, 1996.

Riley, Jason L. *Please Stop Helping Us: How Liberals Make It Harder for Blacks to Succeed*. New York: Encounter Books, 2014.

Ritzema, E. "Truth." In *Lexham Bible Dictionary*, edited by J. D. Barry et al. Logos Software. Bellingham, WA: Lexham, 2016.

Shellenberger, Michael. *Apocalypse Never: Why Environmental Alarmism Hurts Us All*. New York: Harper, 2020.

Solzhenitsyn, Aleksandr. *The Gulag Archipelago*. New York: Harper & Row, 1973.

Sommers, Christina Hoff. *Who Stole Feminism? How Women Have Betrayed Women*. New York: Simon & Schuster, 1995.

Sowell, Thomas. *Discrimination and Disparities*. Rev. and enlarged ed. New York: Basic Books, 2019. [中譯:托馬斯・索维尔著,刘军译:《歧视与不平等》.浙江:江苏出版社,2021.]

Sprinkle, Preston M. *Embodied: Transgender Identities, the Church and What the Bible Has to Say*. Colorado Springs, CO: David C. Cook, 2021.

Trueman, Carl R. *Strange New World: How Thinkers and Activists Redefined Identity and Sparked the Sexual Revolution*. Wheaton, IL: Crossway, 2022.

Williams, Thaddeus J. *Confronting Injustice without Compromising Truth: 12 Questions Christians Should Ask about Social Justice*. Grand Rapids, MI: Zondervan, 2020.

吳弘達:《中國的古拉格:大陸勞改隊及奴工產品眞相》.時報文教基金會叢書.台北:時報文化,1992. (Wu, Hongda Harry. *The Chinese Gulag*. Taipei: Chinese Times Publishing, 1992.)

王礽福:〈蜘蛛女之網:同性戀議題包括甚麼範圍?〉.収《平權?霸權?:審視同性戀議題》,關啟文、戴耀廷、康貴華等著,16-28.香港:天地圖書,2005.

關啟文:《世界怎樣看?怎樣看世界?:基督教世界觀12講》.信仰在場.香港:宣道出版社,2018. (Kwan, Kai-Man. *Twelve Lectures on the Christian Worldview*. Hong Kong: China Alliance Press, 2018.)

關啟文:〈傅柯的權力/真理觀對基督教的挑戰:一個初步的回應〉.収《後現代文化與基督教》,關啟文、張國棟編,183-212.香港:香港基督徒學生福音團契,2002.

關啟文:《同性與變性:評價同性戀運動和變性人婚姻》.信仰在場.香港:宣道出版社,2015. (Kwan, Kai-Man. *Comment on LGBT Movement*. Hong Kong: China Alliance Press, 2015.)

關啟文:〈從自由派到福音派:多馬斯・奧頓的後現代神學〉.於《後現代文化與基督教》,關啟文、張國棟編,347-68.香港:香港基督徒學生福音團契,2002.

關啟文:〈由現代到後現代:一個綜覽〉.於 《後現代文化與基督教》,關啟文、張國棟編,1–16. 香港:香港基督徒學生福音團契, 2002.
關啟文、蔡志森編:《基督教與現代社會的爭論:道德,政治與「宗教右派」》.基督教世界觀叢書.香港:天道書樓, 2012. (Kwan, Kai-man, and Chi-sum Choi, eds. *Christianity and the Debates in Contemporary Society: Morality, Politics, and the Religious Right*. Hong Kong: Tien Dao Press, 2012.)
雷競業、辛惠蘭編:《迎向政治的呼召》.香港:香港基督徒學生福音團契, 2017. (Louie, Kin-yip, and Joyce Sun, eds. *A Call to Political Engagement*. Hong Kong: Fellowship of Evangelical Students, 2017.)

# Faith, Knowledge of "the Faith," and a Journey of Faith

Kenny Lai

## INTRODUCTION

According to the Pew Research Center, there are 2.4 billion Christians worldwide, or about one-third of the world's population. However, the number of Christians in this large group who can be described as Christians "after God's own heart" is unknown. The sign of a true Christian is threefold: faith in Jesus Christ, knowledge of Scripture, and a life of continuous growth. The life of a Christian starts from faith and goes to its end through a journey of faith. This article will discuss the key relationship between faith, knowledge of "the faith" (Jude 1:3)[1], and the growth of spiritual life.

## THE FAITH JOURNEY

Jesus says, "The one who believes has eternal life" (John 6:47). He also says, "I have come so that they may have life, and may have it abundantly" (John 10:10). When a person comes to believe Jesus Christ, at that time he or she has a new life, has a new identity as God's son or daughter, and begins a new journey of faith. All the spiritual characteristics of a Christian, including love, hope, endurance, kindness, etc., start with faith. Throughout the

---

1. NET is used throughout this essay unless otherwise noted.

journey of faith, God is not only with the believer all along the way but also provides his own word as spiritual food, which is the true teaching of the Christian faith.[2]

The journey of faith is both wonderful and challenging. When the path is easy and there are no obstacles, the importance of faith and knowledge of the faith is not obvious; however, they are crucial to standing firm when we are walking on a narrow and rugged path in a valley. How are Christians generally doing on their journey of faith? *Christianity Today* has published surveys regarding the spiritual condition of evangelical Christians in the United States, which showed that a large proportion of believers have a very limited understanding of the Christian faith.[3] Ligonier Ministries, which led the research, concludes, "These results show the pressing need for Christians to be taught Christology, especially as the outcome has gotten worse since 2016."[4] Fred Sanders comments, "This survey indicates that what is at work in many Christians is 'zeal without knowledge.'"[5] Therefore, Christians ought to walk the journey of faith with both sufficient faith and knowledge of doctrine.

Suffering confirms the significance of both faith and knowledge. This world is full of tragedies: incessant wars, cruel murders, torturing hunger, the dissemination of the COVID-19 virus, floods, droughts, fires, earthquakes, and more. Christians are saddened when hearing such news; however, we know the cause of suffering. Suffering is the consequence of sin, so it does not surprise us that the world is full of pain. That being said, when we ourselves are in agony, whether because of the passing away of loved ones, severe illness, financial crisis, or otherwise, we may feel that our faith is not strong enough to bear our great anxiety and stress. In fact, the problem may not be our faith itself but rather our insufficient understanding of

---

2. The Christian faith here can also be thought of as "the body of Christian beliefs." What a Christian believes is the word of God, that is, the truth. Please see the section "The Complete Faith" below.

3. LifeWay Research conducted two surveys for Ligonier Ministries in 2014 and 2018, respectively. There were a total of three thousand people taking part in the surveys, among whom approximately six hundred people were evangelical Christians. Here are the three statements in the surveys and the correspondent responses: (1) "God accepts the worship of all religions," and 51 percent of the respondents agreed. (2) "Jesus was the first creature created by God," and 27 percent of the respondents agreed or did not know. (3) "The Holy Spirit is a force, not a personal being," and 58 percent of the respondents agreed or did not know. Weber, "Christian, What Do You Believe?"; Emmert, "New Poll Finds."

4. Weber, "Christian, What Do You Believe?"

5. Lindgren and Lee, "Our Favorite Heresies of 2018."

Faith, Knowledge of "the Faith," and a Journey of Faith

the Christian faith. I can still remember a believer saying, "Though I believe in Jesus, I do not have a solid knowledge of the Bible, so I often do not know what to do when encountering difficulties in my life." D. A. Carson adds, "For the truth of the matter is that naked beliefs offer little consolation under the worst experience of suffering and evil."[6] Therefore, we believers should endeavor to have a deep understanding of the Christian faith as well as to apply it to real life and to truly live out our faith.

The quality of a Christian's life reflects their faith and knowledge of the faith. The life of a Christian is like a tree, the root of which is his faith, and the source of nutrition is his knowledge of the faith. If the root is strong, the tree can endure harsh weather and still stand firm, and if it is well-nourished, the tree can grow high and vibrant with its leaves green and dense. Likewise, a rich Christian life depends on both steadfast faith and knowledge of the Christian faith.

Faith and knowledge are two sides of a coin. On the one hand, knowledge of the truth builds up a foundation of faith, for without knowledge, faith is weak and empty, collapsing easily from even a little push by the trials of life. As Rom 10:17 says, "Consequently faith comes from what is heard, and what is heard comes through the preached word of Christ"; thus faith that lacks knowledge is a weak faith. On the other hand, one's knowledge has to be built up through faith, for without faith, knowledge is merely a set of propositions in one's mind and does not have any life-renewing efficacy. The author of Hebrews points out that the listener must hear the message with faith, otherwise the message he heard is of no value to him (Heb 4:2). Only through faith can believers benefit from the word of God.[7] Therefore, knowledge that lacks faith is a wooden knowledge. In conclusion, faith and knowledge, complementing and reinforcing each other, together play an indispensable role in a Christian's life. Believers ought to pursue both steadfast faith and holistic knowledge to achieve the fullness of the Christian life.

## THE BEGINNING OF THE FAITH JOURNEY

### The Focal Point of Faith

What is faith? Many would cite Heb 11:1, "Now faith is being sure of what we hope for, being convinced of what we do not see." This verse shows that

---

6. Carson, *How Long, O Lord?*, 20.
7. 馮蔭坤,《希伯來書》, 260.

having faith is to be convinced that what we are now hoping for is unquestionably going to happen in the end, and what we cannot see undoubtedly exists, including things in the past, now, and in the future. How can someone have such great assurance of something he or she has never seen or experienced? The above definition of faith gives the answer. It is not due to the high probability that the thing will happen or does exist. Instead, it is because of one's unreserved confidence that the word and the promises of God Almighty are completely true. Atheists, in the same way, assert that there is no God by virtue of a sort of faith of their own. However, what they believe is data and sometimes speculation. *Therefore, the object of faith is crucial.* Faith reflects one's dependence on what he or she believes, and the depth of faith is commensurate with the degree of that dependence. A person's firm faith is an expression of his firm dependence on what he believes. In Heb 11, the author lists numerous role models of faith and how their lives manifested great faith. This passage not only testifies of their full reliance on God but also reveals that the God in whom they have faith is himself faithful and thus worthy of our faith also. That is why the author affirms, "God is not ashamed to be called their God" (Heb 11:16).

## Saving Faith

The word *faith* has rich meaning, including relying on God and trusting God's word, promises, and power, etc. Among them, the most foundational element is believing God's salvation. Such saving faith is necessary for a person to be saved. One who has saving faith confesses his or her sins, inability to save him- or herself, and need for the atonement of Christ to receive salvation from God. Paul clearly describes saving faith in Rom 10:9–10, "if you confess with your mouth that Jesus is Lord and believe in your heart that God raised him from the dead, you will be saved. For with the heart one believes and thus has righteousness and with the mouth one confesses and thus has salvation." There are two key points about saving faith here. The first is "believe in your heart," which means we truly believe in our hearts that God sent Christ to die and pay the penalty for our sins and later resurrected him from death. When we receive the atonement of Christ, our sins are forgiven, and we are justified by God. The second is "confess with your mouth," which is the external expression of the faith inside our hearts, such as a public statement of our faith.[8] "Confess" means we

---

8. Moo, *Letter to the Romans*, 657.

## Faith, Knowledge of "the Faith," and a Journey of Faith

declare in front of people that Jesus Christ is the Lord of our lives. "Confess with your mouth" cannot be decoupled from "believe in your heart," for "out of the abundance of the heart his mouth speaks" (Luke 6:45). In short, having saving faith means that we believe in our hearts and confess with our mouths that Jesus Christ is both our personal Savior and Lord.

Having saving faith is the beginning of a new life. From then on, the life of God sprouts, grows, and yields fruit in the believer. However, we have observed that some believers do not have assurance of their salvation, which leads to stagnation of their spiritual growth. Other believers consider themselves saved, but in reality, they are still lingering outside the kingdom of God and never enter it. Therefore, having certainty of salvation is so essential to a Christian's life. But how can we achieve that? How can we know that we have saving faith? A common answer is "If you truly confess your sins and repent, receiving Jesus Christ as both your Savior and Lord, you will surely be saved." Or we will say, "Being saved is not a personal feeling but is completely based on God's promise and word," just as Rom 10:9–10 and John 10:27–29 provide "assurance of salvation."[9] Nevertheless, the gap between knowing the Bible verses and applying them to everyday life is analogous to the distance between brain and heart. Though physically they are only around one foot away from each other, their distance is obvious. Therefore, we need to go deeper to understand our true situation to have a right judgment on whether we really have been saved. According to Rom 10:9–10, there are at least three characteristics of saving faith:[10]

1. Acknowledging Christ as the Savior. A person who has saving faith acknowledges that Jesus Christ alone is his Savior and has a good understanding of how Jesus saved him. He always gives thanks to God for his salvation.

2. Honoring Christ. Out of thanksgiving for salvation, the one who has saving faith consistently honors, loves, and endeavors to please Jesus Christ. He or she also puts on the mind and heart of Jesus as the guide to life.

---

9. Jesus says that those who believe in him will also follow him. See Luke 9:23; 14:27; John 8:12; 10:27; 12:26.

10. Bock, "Review of *The Gospel*," 33–34. Bock indicates: "In confessing Jesus as Lord (Rom. 10:9), and coming to Him in faith for salvation, a person is acknowledging that Jesus has authority at three levels: the authority to save, the authority to be honored, and the authority to be followed."

3. Following Christ. A person who has saving faith is willing to follow Christ after he receives Christ as the Savior, for it is appropriate for a servant to follow and serve his lord.

These three characteristics show that a person truly has saving faith. Though the aforementioned attitudes and behaviors might not be fully formed immediately after conversion, they will manifest themselves gradually on the journey. A person who confesses Christ as his Savior and always honors and follows Christ is also willing to know more about him. Thus, he or she is eager to read the Bible and observe God's commandments, just as Jesus says, "The person who has my commandments and obeys them is the one who loves me" (John 14:21).

## ON THE WAY OF THE FAITH JOURNEY

### Faith That Serves

There is a distinctive kind of faith that God gives to believers to build up the church. The Holy Spirit distributes different gifts to each believer as he decides, and at the same time, he also gives out faith for believers to use these gifts, e.g., the faith to prophesy, the faith to perform miracles (Rom 12:6; 1 Cor 12:9; 13:2).[11] Such faith can be classified as *the faith to use gifts*. Paul exhorts believers "not to think more highly of yourself than you ought to think, but to think with sober discernment, as God has distributed to each of you a measure of faith" (Rom 12:3). To put it another way, we receive different measures of faith from the Holy Spirit, through which we use our gifts appropriately and make the most of them. Therefore, we should use our gifts in proportion to the faith given to us. Romans 12 refers to the variety of gifts ("not all the members serve the same function"; "we have different gifts") as well as the single-mindedness of a believer to whom a specific gift is given ("he must . . ."). By saying this Paul seems to imply that it is inappropriate for a believer to serve without the corresponding gift and faith given to him from God, even if he has the will to serve. In other words, for Paul the principle here is not the will of the person, but the gift from God. Take for example a person who has received some gift from the Spirit as well as the faith to use it. If he uses the gift beyond the scope that his faith allows, then it is most likely that something human rather than divine

---

11. 馮蔭坤,《羅馬書註釋》, 2:1714. Fee, *First Epistle to the Corinthians*, 701.

is mixed into the ministry. On the other hand, if he does not use the gift to the extent that his faith grants, that means he does not exert the full power of that gift. Neither of these two scenarios is satisfactory to God. Thus, if a believer has the faith to do one share of work, then let him neither do two shares nor half a share. Using the gift in proportion to the faith is the only way that a believer is able to wield the power of the gift properly and serve along with other church members in harmony.

Then how do we use the gift in accordance with the faith we have received? Paul's answer is "not to think of yourself more highly than you ought to think." First, we should use our gifts humbly, knowing that the Spirit gives us gifts in order to serve each other and we are merely the receiver of the gifts; there is nothing we can boast about. Second, we should appraise with "sober discernment" how we use our gifts and what we have achieved. In this way we can avoid mistaking our own self-confidence as faith received from God. It is also wise to ask people around us for a proper evaluation of our gifts.

## The Complete Faith

The Greek word πίστις is ubiquitous in the New Testament. It has at least two meanings: faith and truth. When used to denote faith, it is usually preceded by an article (ἡ πίστις, the faith); and when it refers to the truth, the Chinese Union Version usually translates it as "道" or "真道" (2 Cor 13:5; 1 Tim 6:21; 2 Tim 4:7). In 1 Timothy, ἡ πίστις and ἡ ἀλήθεια are used interchangeably for many times, indicating that "the faith" is identical to "the truth," which is given to us by God. From 1 Tim 4:1 "some will desert the faith [ἡ πίστις]" and 1 Tim 4:3 "by those who believe and know the truth [ἡ ἀλήθεια]," we can see that the "faith" here refers to the truth.[12] These verses show that a person will deviate from his faith (the truth) if he drifts away from any one of the doctrines. Therefore, staying in the faith means that a person should hold to the full body of Christian doctrine, which is the reason why believers need holistic knowledge of the gospel.

Just as living things do not stop growing, believers also continue to grow. The metaphor of the vine and the branches demonstrates that believers need to remain in Jesus Christ to grow continuously and bear fruit (John 15:4–5). The life-giving connection between vine and branches indicates the

---

12. See 1 Tim 3:9, 13; 4:1, 6; 5:8; 6:10, 12, 21. Also see 1 Tim 2:4, 7; 3:5; 4:3; 6:5 for the understanding of "the truth" (真道).

intimate relationship between believers and Christ while also showing that Jesus's teachings and words have entered the lives of believers (John 15:4). The parable of the four soils depicts varied responses to the gospel and the key to Christian growth. By acquiring the true understanding of the gospel and removing obstacles that hinder growth, a believer can "bear fruit, yielding a hundred, sixty, or thirty times what was sown" (Matt 13:23).

In 1 Tim 4:3, the apostle Paul calls believers "those who believe and know the truth," which implies that, after conversion, believers still need to make progress in faith and endeavor to know more about God. The prophet Jonah did not have a well-rounded understanding of God's character. Though he knew that God always has mercy on gentiles who have repented of their sins, he can hardly believe that God also loves the gentiles who have not yet repented. Therefore, God used a plant to teach Jonah that even gentiles are created by God, and they are cherished by God as well. There are many NT passages that encourage believers to grow up to maturity. For instance, believers should train and build up themselves in the faith (1 Tim 4:6; Jude 1:20), be healthy in the faith (Titus 1:13), and "progress beyond the elementary instructions about Christ and move on to maturity" (Heb 6:1). The apostle Peter exhorts believers to pursue knowing Jesus Christ more intimately, remain firm and established in the truth, and bear fruit to honor God (2 Pet 1:8, 12; 3:18).

Though the world changes, Jesus Christ remains the same forever as do his words, the truth (Heb 13:8). To pursue Christian maturity means that we must wisely use what we have learned in this ever-changing world and apply the principles of Scripture to our daily life. This is by no means easy, so we need to read more books regarding spiritual formation and think more about how current philosophical trends and ideologies challenge our faith and how to respond to these challenges. For instance, postmodernism, which emphasizes moral relativism and self-actualization, is shaking the foundation of traditional marriage and family structure. We have seen a dramatic increase in the divorce rate, and numerous families are falling apart. Moreover, same-sex marriage has become the new normal, and even churches are affected. How shall Christians and churches respond to these trends and accompanying influences? For an individual believer, it is important to understand how to respond biblically through reading and attending discussion forums; for churches, it is beneficial to help congregations to apply biblical principles to the current situation by means of sermons, seminars, and small group discussions. There are also many books reflecting

## Faith, Knowledge of "the Faith," and a Journey of Faith

on ways to achieve Christian maturity; e.g., Ronald Sider brings forth three Cs in Christian marriage (covenant, cross, and community) in responding to the marital crisis in modern society.[13] Nowadays, access to information is more convenient than ever, and believers can have various kinds of ways to learn new things, and even study in a seminary via internet. This is God's special grace for believers in the last days (Dan 12:4).

Paul mentions in Rom 14–15 that some believers are weak in faith and some are strong, which implies that believers may have different levels of understanding regarding the truth during the process of the journey.[14] "Weak in faith" refers to believers who have less knowledge and thus have conflicts and sometimes disputes with those who are more mature, which results in the former's more limited application of faith.[15] However, Paul's focus is on those stronger in faith not passing judgment on those who are weaker. Rather, they should receive their weakness in patience and pursue what makes for peace. On the other side, weaker believers are still asked to keep their faith before God for what they believe despite their incomplete understanding of the truth (Rom 14:5, 6, 22–23). Therefore, we need to encourage the congregation to actively equip themselves in the truth and pursue holistic knowledge with passion. At the same time, though we know that believers will "attain to the unity of the faith and of the knowledge of the Son of God—a mature person" (Eph 4:13),[16] this will not be reached at

---

13. Sider speaks about the importance of the three Cs: "Three biblical truths are essential: Covenant must replace contract; the cross of self-sacrifice must replace personal self-realization; and individualism must give way to community so that the church can offer powerful communal support to marriage and families. These three—covenant, cross, and church community—are the essential Cs for Christian marriage." Sider, *Living Like Jesus*, 48.

14. The "faith" in Rom 14:1 (Τὸν δὲ ἀσθενοῦντα τῇ πίστει; NET, "the one who is weak in the faith") more precisely denotes "knowledge of the faith." For πίστει has the article τῇ, and Paul points to those believers who do not have a holistic understanding of the truth if we inspect the context. Similarly, the "strong" in Rom 15:1 refer to believers who have higher level of understanding of the truth.

15. Here the background is that believers had varied understandings about food and Jewish festivals, for during the transitional period between OT and NT, some of the believers, especially Jewish believers, received the gospel later than their peers in the congregation. A similar case can be found in 1 Cor 8. Paul points out that some believers lack knowledge of the gospel (1 Cor 8:7), for they do not know that all the things are from God, neither do they know that "an idol in this world is nothing." See Cranfield, *Epistle to the Romans*, 2:694–95.

16. "A mature person" (ἄνδρα τέλειον) refers to the church as a whole, i.e., each member of the congregation has well-rounded knowledge of Lord's word, that is, the faith.

once. Continuous effort needs to be made over a long term, lest disputes are raised among the community due to the diverse levels of understanding of the faith.

## The Growing Faith

The faith we hold is not blind but based on concrete facts and can endure various kinds of tests. True faith never stops growing, and this is God's expectation for every believer (2 Cor 10:15; 2 Thess 1:3). There are two ways for faith to grow: one is through increased knowledge of our Lord, including knowledge of the gospel; the other is through real experiences in our lives.

### *Increase Our Knowledge of the Lord*

The level of faith is in proportion to our depth of understanding of the God whom we believe, since we do not trust a stranger but our familiar friends. There are plenty of examples in the Bible to prove this principle. Jesus commends the great faith of the centurion and the Canaanite woman (Matt 8:10; 15:28), for the former knows that Jesus has the power to heal his servant without coming to his house, and the latter realizes that Jesus has grace that abounds even for the gentiles. Both of their understandings go beyond their contemporaries. We recall the disciples, who had followed Jesus for many days and experienced his power but who still panicked when their boat encountered a storm. Jesus reproved them for their little faith because they did not know that Jesus is the Lord of heaven and earth. Jesus even said that they do not have any faith (Mark 4:40). The different behavior in these examples demonstrates that the level of faith is determined by how much a person knows about Christ Jesus. The more we know about Jesus, the greater faith we have in him.

Knowledge of God includes his character, power, promises, etc. As we have mentioned above, the most fundamental faith is saving faith. The starting point for a believer to receive salvation is hearing the gospel, namely, the teachings of Jesus, since faith comes from what is heard. A person needs to hear the gospel, understand it, and receive it to be saved. Similarly, a believer gets to know Christ by understanding his words. Therefore, it is essential for a believer to understand Scripture, that is, Jesus's teaching, and to comprehend the significance of the truth.

## Faith, Knowledge of "the Faith," and a Journey of Faith

The knowledge of Scripture is not only something in the *mind*, but also in the *heart*. There are two reasons that people cannot comprehend the truth. *First, they fail to think carefully and seriously about what they have seen and heard.* For instance, though the disciples experienced Jesus's miracles of feeding thousands of people with very little amounts of food (seven loaves of bread in Mark and five loaves and two fishes in Matthew), they failed to realize that Jesus had the power to create anything *ex nihilo* and still argued about having no bread. So Jesus reproached them because they did not understand, and their hearts had been hardened; they had eyes but did not see, had ears but could not hear, neither did they remember what had taken place right in front of them (Mark 8:17–18).

Interestingly, an unusual "two-stage healing" follows immediately after the disciples' failure of faith. A blind man was brought to Jesus for the healing of his eyes, and only after Jesus placed his hands on the man for the second time was his sight restored. Apparently, the problem was not Jesus's ability, for after Jesus placed his hands on the man again, he "opened his eyes [or 'looked intently'], his sight was restored, and he saw everything clearly." Therefore, the healing of the man is closely related to "the opening of his eyes," which means "looked intently" or "stared with eyes wide open." From this we can see that the man did not look carefully after Jesus first put his hands on him (Mark 8:22–25), and it was his own problem that his eyes were not healed the first time. This narrative reminds us that we should not only read the text of the Bible, but also contemplate what we read to truly understand the life-giving import of its words.

The second reason why a person fails to understand the truth is that *he does not rely on the guidance of the Holy Spirit*. Our Lord gave us the Holy Spirit in our hearts and promised that the Holy Spirit will guide us into all truth (John 16:13), which implies that we need the Spirit to guide (or teach) us to fully understand the word of God.[17] How does the Holy Spirit guide us? We know from Paul's prayer for the Colossians that the Spirit will fill them with the knowledge of God's will in all spiritual wisdom and understanding (Col 1:9).[18] This is not wisdom that comes from the world, but rather the wisdom of Christ, enabling believers to know more about God and thus live their lives in a way that pleases him (Col 1:10; 2:2–3).

---

17. The Greek word ὁδηγέω ("to guide") also has the meaning of "teach." E.g., "The man replied, 'How in the world can I, unless someone guides me?' So he invited Philip to come up and sit with him" (Acts 8:31).

18. Col 1:9: "We continually ask God to fill you with the knowledge of his will through all the wisdom and understanding that the Spirit gives" (NIV).

# Integrating Theology, Church, and Ministry in a Chinese Seminary

Wisdom and understanding of the truth cannot be attained by human effort, and neither should it be sought from the world. They are the special gifts given by the Holy Spirit. Therefore, we should have a proper attitude as we humble ourselves and pray for the guidance of the Spirit to understand the truth as well as live out Christ-like lives.

## *Experience More in Our Lives*

We can see our faith grow also through our real-life experiences in various ways. The first is *practicing the truth*. True faith cannot be separated from works (Jas 2:22); it is not sufficient for one to declare his or her faith merely because he or she has some knowledge or rational understanding. Jesus uses the parable of the two builders (Matt 7:24–27) to demonstrate the difference between the wise man who really practices Jesus's teachings and the foolish man who does not. The former builds his house on rock, whereas the latter on sand. When the rain falls, the flood comes, and the winds beat against the houses, it is clear which one endures this extreme weather. This parable shows that only those who truly live out the truth can endure the winds and storms of their lives. In fact, "understanding" is closely associated with "experience," for only through practicing the truth can one's faith grow steadily and continuously.

The second way for our faith to grow is to *undergo suffering*. No one wants to be afflicted by suffering; however, we have to acknowledge that many believers are going through physical, mental, or spiritual suffering of various kinds, e.g., persecution for the sake of the faith, carrying heavy burdens of ministry, being bedridden due to injury, etc. We know from both Scripture and our own experience that it is inevitable for believers to undergo trials and suffering sooner or later (1 Pet 4:12; 2 Tim 3:12). There are multiple reasons under the surface for afflictions, one of which is that suffering sometimes serves as a means for God to refine our faith. Jesus says, "If anyone wants to become my disciple, he must deny himself, take up his cross daily, and follow me" (Luke 9:23). Acts records the great persecution that the apostle Peter and the disciples endured for the sake of Christ, through which they truly learned what it meant to "share the sufferings of Christ" (1 Pet 4:13). Several times Peter mentions the positive effect of suffering when encouraging believers in various trials. He says, "Such trials show the proven character of your faith, which is much more valuable than gold—gold that is tested by fire, even though it is passing away—and will bring praise and

Faith, Knowledge of "the Faith," and a Journey of Faith

glory and honor when Jesus Christ is revealed" (1 Pet 1:7). Trials make their faith in Christ deeper and firmer. Job did not understand why bad things happened to him, but he nevertheless realized that there is something precious and noble hidden in the disguise of suffering. Thus, he said, "But he knows the pathway that I take; if he tested me, I would come forth like gold" (Job 23:10). David was in agony and desperation during hard times. He cried out, "Why are you depressed, O my soul? Why are you upset?" He prayed to God, "Why do you ignore me?" However, many times in the last verse of a psalm he expresses his full confidence in God, "For I will again give thanks to my God for his saving intervention" (Ps 42:5, 9, 11).

When we are weak in faith, we can pray for help from our Lord. We are familiar with the story of a father whose son is possessed by an unclean spirit and who cried to Jesus to help his unbelief (Mark 9:24). Jesus has mercy on the father and heals his son. More importantly, he teaches him "all things are possible for the one who believes" (Mark 9:23). Although the response of the father is not recorded, it is appropriate to assume that his faith grows because of this incident. When we ask God for faith, God, who always hears prayers, may reveal his almighty work to us immediately and directly or make us go through various trials to refine and deepen our faith. Gideon, who lacked confidence when God sent him to deliver the Israelites, asks God two times for signs of wet and dry fleece to prove that God's promise will be fulfilled. God answers his appeal, using miracles to strengthen Gideon's faith so that he could have the confidence to beat the Midianites. Much has been said about how God builds up believers' faith through trials, yet which means God chooses—miracles or trials—is totally up to his sovereignty.

## THE DESTINATION OF THE FAITH JOURNEY

Jesus's words "be perfect, as your heavenly Father is perfect" point us to the high standard of our heavenly Father, encouraging us to strive for that goal. Although "perfect" (τέλειος) can only be achieved when we meet our Lord in the future, it is conducive to set it as the destination of our faith journey, for we have not only the standard but also the exemplar to imitate, that is, Jesus Christ.

Speaking of the imitation of Christ, Paul says, "Those whom he foreknew he also predestined to be conformed to the image of his Son, that his Son would be the firstborn among many brothers and sisters" (Rom 8:29).

## Integrating Theology, Church, and Ministry in a Chinese Seminary

It is God's will that every believer be conformed to his Son and bear his image. Paul himself is an imitator of Jesus, and he also exhorts believers to be the same (Rom 15:5; 1 Cor 11:1; Phil 3:10; 1 Thess 1:6), imitating his righteousness, kindness, endurance, sacrifice, etc. In fact, we should imitate every character quality of Jesus, for he is perfect without any blemish. His "perfection" is what we should strive to be conformed to.

Paul's exhortation to the church in Colossae explains that the perfection of Christ is the believer's proper goal. He says, "We proclaim him by instructing and teaching all people with all wisdom so that we may present every person mature in Christ" (Col 1:28). The word τέλειος here is very close to the idea in Col 1:22 that God has reconciled believers to himself through the death of Christ to present them holy, without blemish, and blameless before him. From this we can tell that "perfection" is not only about our status in the eyes of God, but also related to judgment in the future (Col 1:22) and the goal that we should pursue in the present (Col 1:23, 28). Paul repeatedly encourages believers in this passage—to remain established and firm in faith (Col 1:23), to know completely the word of God (Col 1:25), to have full assurance (Col 2:2), to be rooted and built up in Christ (Col 2:5, 7)—so we know "perfection" in Paul's writings refers to the constant pursuit of the knowledge of God and the steadfast faith of believers in their whole lives, although we can only attain true "perfection" at the parousia of Christ.[19]

The author of Hebrews makes a similar exhortation but with greater emphasis on maturity in faith. The recipients of the epistle are in danger of apostasy due to persecution. The author points out that one of their problems is their slackness in learning the word of God. As a result, they are still infants and lack the ability to discern good and evil. Therefore, he admonishes them to heed the teachings once given to them and strive for maturity in their faith (Heb 2:1; 5:11—6:1).

The author also encourages them to "hold [their] initial confidence firm until the end" (Heb 3:14; 10:22).[20] He then lists past saints as exemplars of faith, inspiring his readers to imitate those who inherit God's promises

---

19. O'Brien states: "[Paul's] aim is that each one (πάντα ἄνθρωπον) should reach perfection. However, this will be fully realized only on the last day, for only then will they, like the Thessalonian Christians, be completely sanctified." O'Brien, *Colossians-Philemon*, 90.

20. Heb 3:14: "hold fast the beginning of our assurance firm until the end" (NASB). The word ὑπόστασις here denotes "the assured confidence." Heb 10:22: "προσερχώμεθα . . .ἐν πληροφορίᾳ πίστεως," i.e., "let us draw near . . . in full assurance of faith" (NASB).

## Faith, Knowledge of "the Faith," and a Journey of Faith

through faith and perseverance as well as the faith of their leaders who spoke God's message to them (Heb 6:12; 13:7). Most importantly, they should be imitators of Christ. The author of Hebrews says, "We must get rid of every weight and the sin that clings so closely, and run with endurance the race set out for us, keeping our eyes fixed on Jesus, the pioneer and the perfecter of our faith" (Heb 12:1–2). The common understanding of "the pioneer and the perfecter of our faith" is that the faith of believers is initiated and brought to perfection by Jesus. However, the lack of the word "our" in the Greek text indicates that "faith" here does not necessarily refer to believers' faith. In fact, it more likely denotes the faith of Christ from the context, and hence, many translations render the expression as "the pioneer and perfecter of faith" (NIV, NET, NRSV). Moreover, the Greek word ἀρχηγός has multiple meanings, one of the most probable here being "leader," that is, Jesus is the pioneer of the faith.[21] This does not mean that Jesus is leading the way of the faith journey and believers are running after him, but rather that Christ is the epitome of faith and that believers should imitate him, holding the same faith in the heavenly Father. Jesus is at the same time the "perfecter (τελειωτής)" of faith.[22] His whole life on the earth is the perfect manifestation of his faith in the Father, as it is said in Heb 12:2, "For the joy set out for him he endured the cross, disregarding its shame, and has taken his seat at the right hand of the throne of God." His faith has reached its perfection in the suffering of the cross.[23]

If we Christians imitate our Lord, persevering in suffering and not losing our faith, we are on the way to the perfection of faith. The key for us to prevail is our attitude and response toward suffering, knowing that there is positive significance hidden in all the difficulties we have encountered or are undergoing. We should also ponder how great is the suffering that Jesus has endured on the cross, and how unfathomable is the will of God to make his only son suffer to save us.[24] The apostle James says, "My brothers and sisters, consider it nothing but joy when you fall into all sorts of trials, because you know that the testing of your faith produces endurance. And let endurance have its perfect effect, so that you will be perfect and complete,

---

21. 馮蔭坤,《希伯來書》, 2:345.

22. Delling notes: "One who exercises complete faith as demonstrated by suffering, a point which is given such heavy stress in Hebrews." Gerhard Delling, "Τελειωτής," in Kittel and Friedrich, *Theological Dictionary of the New Testament*, 8:87.

23. "In him the faith has reached its perfection." Bruce, *Epistle to the Hebrews*, 338.

24. 葛培理,《浩劫前夕》, 185.

not deficient in anything" (Jas 1:2–4). We cannot entirely circumvent suffering in this life, yet we can choose not to view our suffering negatively. Instead, let us see it from a heavenly perspective, embracing suffering with joy and so reaching the destination of our faith journey without regret.

## BIBLIOGRAPHY

Bock, Darrell L. "A Review of *The Gospel According to Jesus*, by J F MacArthur, Jr, 1988." *Bibliotheca Sacra* 146.581 (Jan. 1989) 21–40.

Bruce, F. F. *The Epistle to the Hebrews*. Rev. ed. New International Commentary on the New Testament. Grand Rapids, MI: Eerdmans, 1990.

Carson, D. A. *How Long, O Lord? Reflections on Suffering and Evil*. Grand Rapids, MI: Baker, 2006.

Cranfield, C. E. B. *A Critical and Exegetical Commentary on the Epistle to the Romans*. Vol. 2. Edited by J. A. Emerton et al. International Critical Commentary. Edinburgh: T&T Clark, 1979.

Emmert, Kevin P. "New Poll Finds Evangelicals' Favorite Heresies." *Christianity Today*, Oct. 28, 2014. https://www.christianitytoday.com/ct/2014/october-web-only/new-poll-finds-evangelicals-favorite-heresies.html.

Fee, Gordon D. *The First Epistle to the Corinthians*. Rev. ed. New International Commentary on the New Testament. Grand Rapids, MI: Eerdmans, 2014.

Kittel, Gerhard, and Gerhard Friedrich, eds. *Theological Dictionary of the New Testament*. Translated by G. W. Bromiley. 10 vols. Grand Rapids, MI: Eerdmans, 1964–76.

Lindgren, Caleb, and Morgan Lee. "Our Favorite Heresies of 2018: Experts Weigh In." *Christianity Today*, Oct. 26, 2018. https://www.christianitytoday.com/news/2018/october/evangelicals-favorite-heresies-ligonier-theology-survey.html.

Moo, Douglas J. *The Letter to the Romans*. 2nd ed. New International Commentary on the New Testament. Grand Rapids, MI: Eerdmans, 2018.

O'Brien, Peter Thomas. *Colossians-Philemon*. Word Biblical Commentary 44. Waco, TX: Thomas Nelson, 1982.

Sider, Ronald J. *Living Like Jesus: Eleven Essentials for Growing a Genuine Faith*. Grand Rapids, MI: Baker, 1996.

Weber, Jeremy. "Christian, What Do You Believe? Probably a Heresy about Jesus, Says Survey." *Christianity Today*, Oct. 16, 2018. https://www.christianitytoday.com/news/2018/october/what-do-christians-believe-ligonier-state-theology-heresy.html.

卡森(D. A. Carson)著,何醇麗譯:《認識苦難的奧祕:苦難冶煉我們對神真正的信心》.神學基礎叢書.台北:校園書房,1997.

葛培理著,陳吳郁娜譯:《浩劫前夕:苦難的透視》.Milltown, NJ:更新傳道會,1985.

馮蔭坤:《希伯來書》.共二卷.天道聖經註釋.香港:天道書樓,1995.

馮蔭坤:《羅馬書註釋》.共二卷.研經叢書.台北:校園書房,2013,三版.

# "Your Heavenly Father Is Perfect"
## Reading the Sermon on the Mount alongside Confucius's *Analects*

### Christopher Chen

> So whatever you wish that others would do to you, do also to them, for this is the Law and the Prophets.
>
> Matthew 7:12

> Do not impose upon others what you do not desire.
>
> Analects 15.24[1]

How do the teachings of Jesus compare to the sayings of other great thinkers?[2] If, as C. S. Lewis has argued, all religions contain "some hint of the truth," how might thoughtful Christians relate the gospel message to the teachings of other philosophies and religions?[3] Undoubtedly, such an endeavor must begin with understanding not only the Bible, but also the works of non-Christian writers. In this essay, I will present one example for reading the Bible alongside one of the great classics of Chinese philosophy. In doing so, I hope to provide a model for Christian cultural engagement

---

1. Unless otherwise noted, this essay uses Edward Slingerland's translation of the *Analects*.

2. A shorter version of this paper was presented at the 2022 Evangelical Theological Society Southwest Regional Meeting. I would like to thank to Jonathan Pennington, Morgan Johnson, and Kevin Chen for providing feedback on earlier versions of this paper.

3. Lewis, *Mere Christianity*, 35.

# Integrating Theology, Church, and Ministry in a Chinese Seminary

and to advance the discussion regarding integration of faith, scholarship, and ministry in Asian contexts.

As the pinnacle of Jesus's teachings, the Sermon on the Mount's timeless message addresses "the good life," which is desired by people across cultures and generations.[4] Although some have read Jesus's teaching alongside its Jewish and Greco-Roman cultural contexts, fewer scholars have read the Sermon against the backdrops of non-Western philosophies.[5] We live in a time when Christianity's center of gravity has moved from the Western hemisphere to Asia, Africa, and Latin America. Gone are the days when we can treat majority world theologies as inherently *contextualized* while viewing Western theology as *normative*.[6] "Every theology is contextual"—though the contextualized nature of Western theology is often overlooked.[7] Considering that cultural contexts act as lenses through which we read (or misread) the Bible, it is important to relate the biblical message to various worldviews.[8] Since many East Asian cultures have been shaped by Confucianism, this paper will discuss Jesus's Sermon in comparison with Confucius's *Analects*.[9]

## THESIS

In this essay, I will argue that while the Sermon on the Mount and the *Analects* address similar ethical topics and often agree upon what constitutes

---

4. Following Jonathan Pennington, I use the word *philosophy* to describe Christianity "as a way of life promising flourishing." Christianity is certainly more than a philosophy, but it is not less than that. Pennington, *Jesus the Great Philosopher*, 21.

5. Pennington, *Sermon on the Mount*, 10–14.

6. Tennent, *Theology in the Context*, 8–9.

7. Yeo, *What Has Jerusalem*, 6.

8. See Richards and O'Brien, *Misreading Scripture*, 12: "Another way of saying this is that all Bible reading is necessarily contextual."

9. Confucianism, Taoism, and Buddhism are the most important traditions in Chinese religion. See Thompson, *Chinese Religion*. For another work that compares the *Analects* with biblical wisdom, see Goh, *Cross-Textual Reading*.

For centuries, Confucius's teachings have influenced the culture and politics of East Asian nations. Although Confucian teaching originated from China, it was very influential during Chosun Korea (1392–1910) and Tokugawa Japan (1600–1868). Confucianism has also deeply influenced Vietnam, Taiwan, Hong Kong, and Singapore.

Today, Confucian values remain at the foundation of Chinese culture, despite efforts to eradicate Confucianism from China during the Cultural Revolution of the mid-twentieth century. Puett, "Who Is Confucius?," 231–36.

"Your Heavenly Father Is Perfect"

virtue, they offer different paths for becoming a virtuous person. Both works appeal to transcendent principles to motivate the pursuit of virtuous lives marked by humble suspicion of public image and the proper use of shame.[10] However, while the *Analects* appeal to *impersonal* transcendent principles (e.g., *dao, tian,* or *li*), the Sermon's ethics are based upon *personal relationship* between disciples and their heavenly Father, who is both the model (Matt 5:48) and rewarder (Matt 6:4, 6, 18) of good deeds. Thus, while the *Analects*'s moral vision lacks a personal transcendent being, Jesus's ethical teachings can be summarized as living a life of integrity that is pleasing to God because "your heavenly father is perfect" (Matt 5:48).[11] In other words, Jesus's repeated emphasis on the heavenly Father is the single most important difference between the Sermon and the *Analects*.

## OUTLINE OF PAPER

In the next two sections I will discuss my methodology and purpose for this comparative study. I will then provide a historical sketch of Confucius and the *Analects* before discussing past encounters between Christianity and Confucianism. Next, I will give an extended discussion of the important themes of heaven and transcendence in the Sermon and the *Analects*, paying special attention to the theme of the heavenly Father as a key distinctive of the Sermon. Lastly, I will discuss the Sermon's ethics through the lens of the *Analects* by focusing on two themes that are common to both works: (1) integrity and public image and (2) the positive use of shame.

## METHODOLOGY

The comparison of the New Testament to other traditions is often done but is not without its difficulties.[12] Comparative studies are always lim-

---

10. For a summary of the positive use of shame in Paul's epistles, see Lau, *Defending Shame*, 172: "Paul uses shame as a pedagogical tool for Christic formation. He engages in honor and shame discourse to cultivate in his readers a dispositional sense of shame that is rooted in the mind of Christ. He also uses shaming rhetoric charged with prospective shame to discourage behavior that dishonors Christ and those for whom Christ died. When his readers persist in sinful behavior, Paul resorts to retrospective shame. He rebukes his readers with the hope that the painful experience of shame will move them to recognize the error of their ways."

11. Unless otherwise noted, the author uses the ESV in this essay.

12. See Barclay and White's survey of these issues in their introductory article "Posing

ited in scope and influenced by the interests of the comparer.[13] As a second-generation Chinese American, I acknowledge my own limitations in grasping the vast "mansion of Confucian philosophy."[14] Despite my limitations, I agree with John Barclay that one fruitful result of the comparative endeavor is to see familiar things in a new light.[15] The act of comparison forces the comparer to defamiliarize their own assumptions, thus opening the possibility of generating new understandings of: (1) their own beliefs and (2) their framework for viewing themselves and others.[16] Although I will inevitably juxtapose the Sermon and the *Analects* to highlight similarities and differences, my goal is to go beyond mere juxtaposition to create new understanding of the Sermon in light of the *Analects*.[17]

## PURPOSE

As an American-born Chinese Christian, I approach both the *Analects* and the Sermon on the Mount with profound appreciation. I affirm that Jesus is the only way (道 *dao*) to the Father (John 14:6), yet I also believe Confucian philosophy offers a helpful backdrop against which one might better understand the gospel.[18] If the gospel is like a multifaceted gemstone, its beauty can be observed more clearly when placed alongside various cultural backdrops.[19] While the gospel can become too familiar when viewed from a monocultural perspective, one's understanding of the gospel can be

---

the Questions," 1–8.

13. See Smith, *Drudgery Divine*, 51: "In the case of the study of religion, as in any disciplined inquiry, comparison, in its strongest form, brings differences together within the space of the scholar's mind for the scholar's own intellectual reasons."

14. In the words of the Chinese philosopher Lin, *From Pagan to Christian*, 67–68, "If I write about the mansion of Confucian philosophy now, I am aware that thousands of Chinese scholars have done some before me; still I can write only of my own perceptions and insights and my own evaluations and interpretations."

15. Barclay, "'O wad some Pow'r,'" 9–22.

16. In this work, I argue not for a genealogical connection between Jesus's Sermon on the Mount and Confucius's *Analects* but rather an analogical comparison between the two traditions.

17. By stating my purpose here, I aim to heed the warning in Smith, *Drudgery Divine*, 53: "Lacking a clear articulation of purpose, one may derive arresting anecdotal juxtapositions or self-serving differentiations, but the disciplined constructive work of the academy will not have been advanced, nor with the study of religion have come of age."

18. See, for example, Ten Elshof, *Confucius for Christians*.

19. See, for example, Lau, *Politics of Peace*.

infused with "new energy from other cultures."[20] Thus, careful comparison can illuminate previously underemphasized contours of the gospel.

At its best, Christianity has flourished when transplanted into various cultural and philosophical environments.[21] In the Sermon on the Mount, Jesus juxtaposed his teachings against a Jewish worldview through his sixfold formula "you have heard that it was said . . . but I say to you" (Matt 5:21–48).[22] At Athens, Paul dialogued with Greek philosophers (Acts 17:18–21). Though Paul's aims were evangelistic, he modeled how to bring the gospel into dialogue with other philosophies. As K. K. Yeo explains, "Through dialogue, the gospel is indigenized by the use of native words, concepts, and expressions."[23] Like Paul, one of my aims is to encourage Christians to understand the *Analects* and to relate the gospel message to its adherents. Thus, I will seek to present the *Analects* in an evenhanded and respectful way.[24] In summary, my purposes are twofold: (1) to better understand the Sermon on the Mount by viewing it in comparison with the *Analects* and (2) to foster constructive dialogue with the goal of presenting the Sermon's message in a compelling way to adherents of Confucianism.

## CONFUCIUS AND THE *ANALECTS*: A HISTORICAL SKETCH[25]

### Confucius's Life and Times

Confucius lived during the years 551–479 BC during the Spring and Autumn periods of the Eastern Zhou Dynasty (1046–256 BC).[26] The Eastern Zhou Dynasty was marked by a gradual decline in the power of the Zhou kings,

---

20. Zhao, *Father and Son in Confucianism*, x.

21. Jesus's incarnation exemplifies the beauty of a heavenly Word embodied in human flesh (John 1:14). In the Chinese Union Version, John 1:14 reads "the *dao* [the Way] became flesh" (道成了肉身).

22. Lawrence, *Comparative Characterization*, 1–6.

23. Yeo, *What Has Jerusalem*, 190. He elaborates, "Even Paul's Areopagus speech, which is a mission speech with the intention of conversion, is not itself a monologue. The fact that he uses much of the cultural, social, and literary material of the audience indicates the forum or dialogue in progress between the rhetor and the audience" (189–90).

24. Yao, *Confucianism and Christianity*, 1–5.

25. For a helpful brief introduction to Confucius and the *Analects* see Slingerland, Analects, xiii–xxvi; Ni, *Understanding the* Analects, 1–29. For book length treatments, see Gardner, *Confucianism*; Goldin, *Confucianism*; Yao, *Introduction to Confucianism*.

26. In this paragraph, I rely heavily on Slingerland's introductory material in Slingerland, Analects, xx.

with local feudal lords and ministers gradually rising to power. By the time of Confucius's birth, the Zhou kings had become mere figureheads while even the local feudal lords were losing their power to upstart ministers. Although little is known about the life of Confucius, he apparently came from a humble economic background and belonged to the scholar-official class. Confucius famously described his own spiritual autobiography in a few brief sentences showing progression from learning to application as he matured in age (*Analects* 2.4).[27] By age seventy, Confucius claimed to have reached a state where his inner desires were consistent with proper behavior.

## Overview of the *Analects*

The *Analects* are divided into twenty books, which are further subdivided into verses. Each verse presents brief wisdom sayings either directly from Confucius or as a conversation between "the Master" and his various disciples.[28] Though the verses appear without historical background and often seem disconnected from one another, several key themes recur, including: humaneness (仁 *ren*), filial piety (孝 *xiao*), virtue (德 *de*), heaven (天 *tian*), the way (道 *dao*), righteousness (義 *yi*), and ritual propriety (禮 *li*).[29] Though each of these themes could merit a lengthy discussion on its own, I will later choose to focus upon the theme of heaven (*tian*) as a helpful point of contact for comparison to the Sermon on the Mount.[30]

---

27. The linear progression of ethical maturity is consistent with Confucius's emphasis on respect for elders. If wisdom took seventy years for Confucius to master, how audacious would it be for a young person to claim more wisdom than his elders?

28. Like the Sermon, the *Analects* also mentions and improves upon previously known sayings which were common knowledge to their hearers. Addressing an audience familiar with the law of Moses, Jesus repeatedly employed his classic formula, "You have heard it said . . . but I say to you" to adjust his hearers' understanding of the law. Confucius employed a similar approach by responding to his disciples' understanding of common sayings. For example, in book 12, the disciple Zixia approaches the Master saying, "I have heard it said . . ." (*Analects* 12.5) to preface a statement for which he would like to gain insights from the Master.

29. Ni, *Understanding the* Analects, 31–75.

30. The *Analects* and the teachings of Jesus could also be studied for their different representations of other shared terms such as *righteousness* (義 *yi*), *joy* (樂 *le*), *harmony* (和 *he*), or *educated person* (士 *shi*).

"Your Heavenly Father Is Perfect"

# Reception History of the *Analects*

The *Analects* has had a long and complex reception history as the Confucian tradition found varying degrees of acceptance throughout the history of China. Until the Qin Dynasty (221-206 BC) the two most influential proponents of Confucian teaching were Mengzi (or "Mencius," fourth century BC) and Xunzi (298-238 BC). While Mengzi developed Confucian thought toward an ethical and religious direction, Xunzi emphasized humanistic rationalism. By the Song Dynasty (906-1279) Mengzi would become regarded as "the only orthodox transmitter of the ancient culture after Confucius himself."[31] Although Confucianism was eclipsed by Buddhism during the Sui (581-618) and Tang (618-907) Dynasties, it nevertheless continued to influence Chinese thought and was officially revived during the Song Dynasty (906-1279) through the neo-Confucian movement.[32] During the Ming Dynasty (1368-1644), the *Analects* became part of the basis of China's civil service examination, ensuring that it would have been memorized by every educated Chinese person from 1313 until the last nationwide exam in 1910. Similar national exams in Japan, Korea, and Vietnam ensured that the *Analects* would play a critical role in the formation of East Asian culture.

## CHRISTIAN ENCOUNTERS WITH CONFUCIANISM

Christians have a long history of encounters with Confucianism. The works of Confucius were first translated from Chinese into Latin by Jesuit scholars.[33] Jesuit missionary Matteo Ricci (1552-1610) studied the Confucian classics with the goal of conversing using terms that were common to Chinese culture.[34] While Ricci was more hostile toward Buddhism (which he viewed as a competing religion), he had more sympathy for Confucianism.[35] Indeed, Ricci saw Confucianism as "primarily an ethic, a moral and a social philosophy, needing complementing and clarifying, but basically sound from a Christian point of view."[36] By seeking to blend

---

31. Yao, *Introduction to Confucianism*, 71-72.
32. Slingerland, Analects, xxiv-xxv.
33. Meynard, *Jesuit Reading of Confucius*.
34. Young, *Confucianism and Christianity*, 25-39.
35. Rule, "Jesuit and Confucian?," 117-22.
36. Rule, "Jesuit and Confucian?," 114.

## Integrating Theology, Church, and Ministry in a Chinese Seminary

Confucianism with Christianity, Ricci claimed to follow Aquinas's model of synthesizing Aristotelian philosophy with Christian revelation. In Ricci's view, Confucianism was "based on a natural religion, true so far as it goes but incomplete in its view of God and man."[37] Thus, Ricci stressed that "Confucianism is a *philosophy*, not a rival theology to Christianity but a purely rational system."[38] Though some would accuse Ricci of syncretism, others suggest that Ricci embraced Confucianism while stopping short of syncretism.[39]

Was Ricci right to suggest that Confucianism is "sound from a Christian point of view" except that it is "incomplete in its view of God and man"? Regardless of one's faith commitments, such an oversimplified assessment seems to risk flattening out the differences between the Christian and Confucian worldviews. At the same time, Ricci was right to appreciate that there are points of continuity between Confucian and Christian teaching. But did he go too far? Indeed, Christians living in East Asian contexts have faced a perennial challenge of how to articulate the gospel in categories that are understandable to adherents of a Confucian worldview. At the opposite end of the spectrum from Ricci, some have tended to propagate what Gregg Ten Elshof calls a "Western Christianity—Christianity articulated in categories and with emphases at home in the Western philosophical tradition."[40] Thus, difficulties arise when a cultural Confucian is "asked to not only embrace Christian thinking, but to abandon their native Confucian wisdom tradition."[41]

In the early part of the twentieth century, Chinese Christian academics sought to present the Christian truth in ways that were familiar to Confucian thinkers. One of these academics was Wu Leichuan, who published a series of books on the Sermon on the Mount during in the 1920s. Although Wu rightly recognized the centrality of the Lord's prayer in the Sermon,

---

37. Rule, "Jesuit and Confucian?," 123.

38. Rule, "Jesuit and Confucian?," 123 (emphasis original).

39. Rule, "Jesuit and Confucian?," 122. Rule defends the Jesuit missionary by suggesting that Ricci was seeking "to found a Chinese Christian theology; not just a Chinese Christian church."

40. Ten Elshof, *Confucius for Christians*, 3.

41. Ten Elshof, *Confucius for Christians*, 3–4. Ten Elshof points out that Western audiences do not typically face such stark choices since the gospel is often articulated in ways that do not require "wholesale abandonment of the rich wisdom tradition that stretches back to Socrates and Plato and informs the most fundamental structures of life and social interaction in the West."

his theologically liberal tendencies led him to focus on the brotherhood of humans rather than the relationship between disciples and their heavenly Father.[42] As the twentieth century progressed, Chinese Christians seemed to give less attention to the Sermon as theologically conservative preachers focused upon regeneration, justification, and conversion.[43] Sadly, the ethical teachings of the Sermon seemed to receive less attention in Chinese Christian thought. Having provided a brief overview of Christian encounters with Confucianism, I will now show how the message of the Sermon can be better appreciated when brought into dialogue with the *Analects*.

## HEAVEN AND TRANSCENDENCE IN THE SERMON AND THE *ANALECTS*

The Sermon on the Mount presents the kingdom of heaven as an otherworldly paradigm to motivate disciples toward virtuous behavior.[44] Indeed, Jesus freely employed the language of heaven (and hell) and eternal rewards (and punishment), while Confucius was reticent to comment upon metaphysics or the afterlife.[45] At the same time, Confucius also referred to heaven (*tian*) as a transcendent reality to motivate ethical behavior. In this section, I will explore the related themes of heaven and transcendence in the Sermon and the *Analects*. While both works refer to heaven, a critical difference between the two is that Confucius viewed heaven as an impersonal principle while Jesus focused his disciples' attention on a personal relationship with their heavenly Father.

### *Shangdi* and *Tian* in Chinese Thought

Confucius lived during a time of fluidity regarding Chinese belief in a personal deity. Archaeological and textual evidence from the Shang Dynasty (1751–1122 BC) suggest that the Chinese formerly believed in a supreme heavenly ruler (上帝 *shangdi*, Lord above).[46] By the time of the Zhou Dy-

---

42. Yieh, "Reading the Sermon," 146–47.

43. Yieh, "Reading the Sermon," 158–59.

44. By comparison, some have characterized the teachings of Confucius's *Analects* as a path of humanistic self-realization. Chang, *Asia's Religions*, 40.

45. Hall and Ames, *Thinking through Confucius*, 24; Chang, *Asia's Religions*, 24–25.

46. Whereas the emperor was known as *di*, the heavenly emperor was known as *shangdi*.

nasty, however, the term *shangdi* was replaced by the depersonalized title *tian* (heaven).[47] For the Chinese, "heaven" (*tian*) refers to "an anthropomorphic figure—someone who can be communicated with, angered, or pleased—rather than a physical place."[48] Although scholars debate the exact connotations of *shangdi* and *tian*, Laurence Thompson rightly asserts that the Chinese "Supreme Ruler in heaven, although the highest deity, is not equivalent to the God of Western religion or philosophy."[49] Moreover, Peimin Ni explains that *shangdi* is not viewed as the transcendental deity who created the universe, but is instead an "anthropomorphic extension of ancestral veneration," which could be more appropriately rendered as "supreme ancestral emperor." Compared to *shangdi*, "*Tian* is even further away from the Judeo-Christian notion of transcendental God."[50]

## Heaven (*Tian*) and Transcendence in the *Analects*

In the *Analects*, the concept of *tian* is the closest parallel to "heaven" in the Sermon on the Mount. Confucian scholars hold varying opinions on whether *tian* is personal or impersonal and whether it is transcendent or immanent.[51] While some hold that *tian* is anthropomorphic, they nevertheless distinguish it from Western conceptions of a deity who exists apart from matter.[52] Indeed, how one understands *tian* relates to one's views on immanence and transcendence in Confucianism. On the one hand, Confucian scholars David Hall and Roger Ames have argued that early Confucianism lacks a transcendent principle in its worldview.[53] As Hall and Ames point out, "Confucius as portrayed in the *Analects* seems to express an ambivalence toward, if not a cultivated disinterest in, cosmological

---

47. Thompson, *Chinese Religion*, 2–3.
48. Slingerland, Analects, xviii.
49. Thompson, *Chinese Religion*, 3.
50. Ni, *Understanding the* Analects, 41.
51. Ni, *Understanding the* Analects, 41.
52. Hall and Ames, *Thinking through Confucius*, 204–8.
53. Hall and Ames, *Thinking through Confucius*, 12–13. For Hall and Ames, Confucius's original writings focus on the "radical immanence" of the cosmos, while his later interpreters saw a transcendent principle in Confucius's writings. Hall and Ames rightly characterize their own views as "uncommon" among Confucian scholars. While their work has stimulated much scholarly discussion, they are not without their critics. See, for example, Wilson, "Conformity, Individuality," 271–74.

speculations."[54] John Berthrong disagrees with Hall and Ames, agreeing with neo-Confucian scholar Chu Hsi that *li* (principle) can be understood as "the transcendent order of the world."[55] Shu-hsien Liu explains that while *li* was not an important idea in early Confucianism, *li* developed into perhaps the most important concept in Chinese philosophy beginning in the Northern Song period (960–1127) partly due to the influence of Buddhism.[56] Liu's view is consistent with Hall and Ames' assertion that transcendence was a later development of the Confucian tradition and not part of Confucius's original teaching.[57]

However, if transcendence was a subsequent development after the time of Confucius, it may have developed quite early in the Confucian tradition. Mencius (fourth century BC), the influential early interpreter of Confucius, viewed *tian* as transcendent. For Mencius, "Nothing is higher than *tian*, and so *tian* is transcendent" and the mandate of heaven (天命 *tian ming*) is a transcendent power.[58] However, unlike Plato and Aristotle who divided reality into the transcendent realm and the realistic world, Mencius did not seem to view the transcendent *tian* as external to human beings. Confucianist scholar Yijie Tang explains that "Mencius conceived of *tian-dao* (the way of heaven) and *ren-dao* (the way for human beings) in unity."[59]

Other scholars see *dao* (the Way) or *tian dao* (天道 the Way of Heaven) as the transcendent principles within Confucianism. Readers hold a variety of interpretations of *tian dao*, a phrase that only appears once in

---

54. Hall and Ames, *Thinking through Confucius*, 196. For more details on Confucius's cosmology, see chapter 4 of Hall and Ames where the authors discuss transcendence as it relates to *tian* (204–8), *tian ming* (208–16), *de* (216–26), and *dao* (226–32).

55. Berthrong, *All under Heaven*, 88.

56. Liu, "Li: Principle, Pattern, Reason."

57. Hall and Ames, *Thinking through Confucius*, 24: "This relationship between the original teachings of Confucius and the later interpretations can be understood in two ways. Either Confucius, for whatever reason, has been used as a medium to conceal the novel ideas of innumerable creative individuals, or he is in fact a 'corporate' person who is continually being seen in a new way by virtue of the participation of later thinkers in the ongoing transmission of cultural values. Thus viewed, 'Confucius' is a community, a society, a living tradition."

58. Tang, "Transcendence and Immanence," 175.

59. Tang, "Transcendence and Immanence," 175, who then cites Mencius's words, "A sincere person follows a way, [but] he has to understand what is good, otherwise he cannot embody sincerity. Hence sincerity is the way of heaven; the very thought of sincerity is the way of human beings."

the *Analects* (*Analects* 5.13).[60] When *dao* appears elsewhere in the *Analects*, it seems to transcend humans, inviting conformity to its ideals (*Analects* 15.29). Slingerland summarizes, "The Way thus is transcendent, in the sense that it continues to exist even when it is not being actively manifested in the world, but it requires human beings to be fully realized."[61]

Confucian scholar Mou Zongsan views "the intrinsic connection between the outer transcendence of heaven (*tian*) and the inner transcendence of human nature (*xing*) as the Confucian ideal."[62] For Mou, the mandate of heaven (*tianming*) is fulfilled in the unity of heaven and humans (*tianren heyi*, 天人合一), which is achieved through moral cultivation of *ren* (humaneness, 仁). For Mou, the goal of Confucianism is "perichoretic relationship between the human and nonhuman worlds."[63] This harmonious ideal could be attained only through human moral effort.[64]

Hall and Ames are correct to point out Confucius's reticence to explain transcendent matters (*Analects* 5.13, 7.21). However, there is sufficient evidence in the *Analects* to suggest that Confucius believed in a transcendent principle, whether that be *tian* (heaven), *dao* (the Way), or *li* (principle). By eschewing detailed explanations of the transcendent, Confucius focused his disciples' attention on "what was within human control: commitment to learning and the Confucian Way."[65] Even though he avoided speculations about the transcendent, Confucius clearly acknowledged the existence of a transcendent way (*dao*, *Analects* 15.29), heavenly way (*tian dao*, *Analects* 5.13), and heavenly mandate (*tian ming*, *Analects* 2.4). As Tang points out, at the heart of Confucian philosophy is the paradoxical "realization of immanent transcendence."[66]

---

60. *Analects* 5.13 is also one of only two places in the *Analects* where human nature (*xing*) is mentioned (cf. *Analects* 17.2). For more on the history of interpretation of *Analects* 5.13, see Ivanhoe, "Whose Confucius? Which Analects?," 119–33.

61. Slingerland, *Analects*, 186.

62. Yeo, "Logos and Pneuma of Creation," 150.

63. Yeo, "Logos and Pneuma of Creation," 150.

64. Yao, *Confucianism and Christianity*, 31.

65. Slingerland, *Analects*, 45.

66. Tang, "Transcendence and Immanence," 175. He adds, "That is to say, *tian-dao* is not only transcendent but immanently transcendent. Similarly, *ren-xing*, human nature as it should be, is not only immanent but transcendent, and is itself also immanently transcendent."

## "Your Heavenly Father Is Perfect"

Some, such as the Christian academic Lin Yutang, have gone so far as to suggest that Confucius believed in a personal God.[67] However, given that the impersonal *tian* (heaven) had replaced the personal *shangdi* (Lord above) during the Zhou dynasty, it seems unlikely that Confucius believed in a monotheistic God.[68] Thus, although Confucius believed in prayer to spirits and to heaven (*Analects* 3.13), there is very little evidence in the *Analects* to suggest that Confucius believed *tian* was a personal God. Although heaven (*tian*) is at times characterized as governing natural order (*Analects* 17.19), *tian* is nevertheless portrayed as nonverbal and impersonal.[69]

Regardless of the position one takes concerning the transcendence of *tian*, *dao*, or *li*—it seems fair to suggest that the ethics of the *Analects* are not based upon human relationship with a *personal* transcendent being. Paulos Huang summarizes: "Although many neo-Confucians agreed that Heaven can govern the world, they neither thought Heaven has personality nor that it transcends the world and human rationality."[70] It is at this point that our understanding of the *Analects* can help us to better appreciate an important distinctive of the Sermon on the Mount.

## Heaven in the Gospel of Matthew

The Gospel of Matthew is distinct in its emphasis upon the dual themes of heaven and earth.[71] Throughout his Gospel, Matthew uses heaven and earth to emphasize "the antithesis between God and humanity" while focusing on "the tension between the two realms as well as the eschatological goal of their reunification (cf. 6:9–10; 28:18)."[72]

The singular and plural forms of οὐρανός (heaven, heavens) appear 82 times in Matthew, accounting for 30 percent of their appearances in the New Testament.[73] The theme of heaven is particularly prevalent in the

---

67. Lin Yutang reads "Heaven's Mandate" (*tian dao*) in *Analects* 2.4 as the "will of God." Lin, *From Pagan to Christian*, 74.

68. Thompson, *Chinese Religion*, 2–3.

69. In one notable passage on *tian*, Confucius said, "What does Heaven ever say? Yet the four seasons are put in motion by it, and the myriad creatures receive their life from it. What does heaven ever say?" (*Analects* 17.19). Ni, *Understanding the* Analects, 42, argues that *tian* here is immanent, though does not make the case that *tian* is personal.

70. Huang, *Confronting Confucian Understandings*, 178.

71. Pennington, *Heaven and Earth in Matthew*.

72. Pennington, *Heaven and Earth in Matthew*, 216.

73. Pennington, *Heaven and Earth in Matthew*, 125–26. The singular and plural

Sermon on the Mount, where the singular or plural forms of οὐρανός appear 18 times. Since the theme of *tian* (heaven) is also prevalent in the *Analects*, what features (if any) set the Sermon apart from the *Analects*? The most fundamental difference between the two works is that the ethics of the Sermon are based upon a disciple's personal relationship with the transcendent heavenly Father.

## The Heavenly Father in the Sermon

As a subset of the "heaven" theme, the "heavenly Father" is a significant subtheme in Matthew's Gospel.[74] The Gospels refer to God as "father" over 170 times, with the greatest concentration in John (109 times) and Matthew (44 times). In Matthew's Gospel, the highest concentration of references to God as "father" occurs in the Sermon (17 times, including 10 times in Matt 6:1–21).[75] Moreover, all instances of "father" in the Sermon emphasize personal relationship with God by calling him "*your* father" (15 times), "*our* father" (1 time), or "*my* father" (1 time).[76]

The heavenly Father is indeed a crucial theme of the Sermon, leading Ulrich Luz to suggest that "righteousness" and "father" are two key words that "indicate the subject-matter of the Sermon."[77] Scholars typically suggest that the Father's transcendence and intimacy are emphasized by describing him as the *heavenly* Father. While transcendence is a significant aspect of the Father's identity, the "heavenly" descriptor can also be connected to the broader themes of heaven and earth in Matthew's Gospel.[78] The "in heaven" descriptor of the Father emphasizes that "God rules over all and is distinct from the earth."[79] As Robert Foster points out, heavenly language serves multiple purposes (rhetorical, sociological, and theological) within the Sermon on the Mount.[80]

---

forms of οὐρανός appear 273 times in the Greek New Testament. At 82 appearances, Matthew's Gospel has more occurrences than any other biblical book in the Greek New Testament or the Septuagint.

74. Pennington, *Heaven and Earth in Matthew*, 231–51.
75. Pennington, *Heaven and Earth in Matthew*, 242.
76. Pennington, *Heaven and Earth in Matthew*, 231–32.
77. Luz, *Theology of Matthew*, 3.
78. Pennington, *Heaven and Earth in Matthew*, 234–36.
79. Pennington, *Heaven and Earth in Matthew*, 251.
80. Foster, "Why on Earth," 487–99.

"Your Heavenly Father Is Perfect"

In Matt 5:48, the heavenly Father is presented as the model for Christian ethics. Elsewhere in the Sermon, Jesus repeatedly emphasizes that the disciples have a heavenly Father who cares for their needs (Matt 6:26, 33; 7:11). The Sermon also characterizes the heavenly Father as the rewarder of good deeds done in secret (Matt 6:4, 6, 18) to motivate disciples to live out a counter-cultural ethic. Thus, Jesus pointed the disciples to "look toward heaven for their standard of righteousness, their strength for holy living, and their reward for their labours."[81] Throughout the Sermon, Jesus's ethical teachings are firmly rooted upon the character of the heavenly Father. There are just two ways of living: for the praise of humans or for rewards from the heavenly Father.[82]

## Viewing the Heavenly Father of the Sermon through the Lens of the *Analects*

Like the Sermon, the *Analects* also emphasizes the importance of the father-son relationship. The *Analects* teach esteem for one's human father expressed through *xiao* (respect) and *li* (rites) during the father's life, death, and burial (*Analects* 2.5; cf. 1.2, 1.6, 1.11). During the time of Confucius, respect for elders was commonly displayed through ritual sacrifices to one's deceased parents. However, Confucius shifted the emphasis of filial piety from honoring one's dead ancestors toward honoring one's living parents (*Analects* 11.11).[83] According to the *Analects*, a virtuous son would limit his travels to avoid neglecting his filial duties (*Analects* 4.19). Children were called to serve their parents (*Analects* 4.18) and to avoid doing anything that would cause parental anxiety (*Analects* 2.6). Filial piety meant allowing elders to eat first at mealtimes—but it certainly went beyond such actions (*Analects* 2.8). In summary, one scholar explains that in early Confucianism, filial piety centered around respectful care, obedience, and moral vigilance.[84]

Given the importance of the father-son relationship in the *Analects*, the heavenly Father can be a helpful image to explain the Sermon to people from a Confucian background.[85] Whereas the *Analects* focus on piety to-

81. Foster, "Why On Earth," 499.
82. Pennington, *Heaven and Earth in Matthew*, 247.
83. Zhao, *Father and Son in Confucianism*, 21–22.
84. Roetz, *Confucian Ethics of the Axial Age*, 53.
85. For another perspective on relating God the Father to Confucianism, see Lee, *Trinity in Asian Perspective*, 124–50.

ward human parents without appealing to a personal transcendent being, the Sermon presents the heavenly Father who calls believers into a loving relationship and whose authority supersedes even that of human parents. This relationship is not marked by merely *xiao* (respect) and *li* (ritual) but a tender bond between Father and child (Matt 6:9; cf. 11:28). Moreover, at several points in Matthew's Gospel, Jesus "calls his disciples to make a decisive choice between their fathers and his heavenly father (Matt 8:21; 10:34–37; 23:29–32)."[86] While it is right to honor one's earthly parents (Eph 6:2), the heavenly Father calls for wholehearted allegiance and obedience. This relationship can be summarized in the call to imitate the heavenly Father by being "perfect as your heavenly father is perfect" (Matt 5:48).

## What Does It Mean to Be Like God?

Like the *Analects*, the Sermon presents a pathway to wisdom.[87] However, instead of motivating his disciples using impersonal forces as in the *Analects*, Jesus's wisdom is based upon an intimate relationship with the heavenly Father. Thus, Jesus's way of life is in continuity with the message of Old Testament wisdom literature, which emphasizes that "the fear of the Lord is the beginning of wisdom" (Prov 1:8).[88] Indeed, the ethics of the Hebrew Scriptures are based on a covenantal "*relationship* . . . characterized by relating to God and each other in ways that accord with God's own nature."[89]

To say that Christian ethics is unique in that it derives its principles from God may be a bit too vague to be of help. As Christopher Wright contends, we must "be more specific about the word 'God'" and in what sense we are to derive our ethics from him.[90] Thus, to "be perfect as your heavenly father is perfect" (Matt 5:48) means to become people whose thoughts and

---

86. Pennington, *Heaven and Earth in Matthew*, 249.
87. Pennington, *Sermon on the Mount*, 19–40.
88. Longman, *Fear of the Lord*, 5–25. Pennington, *Sermon on the Mount*, 37.
89. Pennington, *Jesus the Great Philosopher*, 47 (emphasis original). Pennington points out that this relational aspect is what sets the Hebrew Bible apart from other ethics in the ancient world, including Greco-Roman ethics. On 48, he adds, "What distinguishes the Hebrew Scripture's virtue ethic from others in the ancient world is its focus on this ethic coming through the revelation of a personal, covenantal God."
90. Wright, *Old Testament Ethics*, 24. Wright then goes on to explain how biblical ethics is based upon a believer's response of gratitude toward the identity, character, grace, and redeeming actions of God as described in the pages of Scripture. Wright, *Old Testament Ethics*, 24–32.

actions reflect the heavenly Father's identity, character, grace, and actions. Such an ethic is both "imitative" (disciples are to imitate God) and "agentic" (who we are as people matters).[91]

However, what does it mean to imitate God the Father? Wright explains that imitating God does not mean "mere mimickry—attempting to do *whatever* the Lord did or does, for clearly there are whole areas of the activity of God that are not available or appropriate for human replication."[92] Just as the New Testament's instructions toward Christlikeness do not mean that Christians can or should mimic every detail of Jesus's behavior, so likewise imitating God must mean something more nuanced than mere mimicry. Rather than aping behavior, biblical ethics is about acting in ways that are consistent with God's character.[93] In other words, the Sermon calls disciples to be like God in *character*.[94] Since the call to character formation is central to both the *Analects* and the Sermon, in the next section, I will explain how the *Analects* can provide a helpful lens through which to view the Sermon's ethics.

## THE SERMON'S ETHICS THROUGH THE *ANALECTS*' LENS

The Sermon and the *Analects* can naturally be compared from the perspective of virtue ethics, which emphasizes the importance of character and motives behind one's external behavior.[95] Confucian scholar Antonio S. Cua helpfully summarizes: "Throughout its long history, Confucianism has stressed character formation or personal cultivation of virtues, *de*. Thus it seems appropriate to characterize Confucian ethics as an ethics of virtues."[96] The virtue ethics of the *Analects* is reflected in verses such as

---

91. Pennington, *Jesus the Great Philosopher*, 75.

92. Wright, *Old Testament Ethics*, 37 (emphasis original).

93. For this reason, Wright prefers to describe biblical ethics as acting in a way that *reflects* God's character, rather than simply copying God's actions.

94. This call to character forms the foundation for the commands to be like God in both the Old Testament (Lev 19:2) and the Sermon on the Mount (Matt 5:48).

95. Pennington, *Sermon on the Mount*; Pennington, *Jesus the Great Philosopher*, 75–76; Cua, "Confucianism: Ethics"; Slingerland, "Virtue Ethics, the 'Analects,'" 97–125; Slingerland, "Situationist Critique," 390–419.

96. Cua, "Confucianism: Ethics," 73. Cua adds two important clarifications: "First, the Confucian focus on the centrality of virtues assumes that *de* can be rendered as 'virtue.' Second . . . this focus does not depreciate the importance of rule-governed conduct or the principled interpretation of basic notions."

Integrating Theology, Church, and Ministry in a Chinese Seminary

this one: "Virtue is never solitary; it always has neighbors" (*Analects* 4.25). Similarly, in the Sermon on the Mount, Jesus calls his disciples to a greater righteousness that exceeded the externalism of the scribes and Pharisees (Matt 5:20). In this section I will examine two key themes in the Sermon and the *Analects*: (1) integrity and public image and (2) the positive use of shame. In each subsection, I will briefly highlight instances where the *Analects* addresses the theme. I will then show how reading the Sermon alongside the *Analects* can help illuminate the message of the Sermon.

## Integrity and Public Image

Both the Sermon and the *Analects* emphasize integrity and public image, drawing special attention to one's motivations for doing public acts. The *Analects* prescribe wariness of outward appearances (*Analects* 11.21) and warn that "a clever tongue and fine appearance are rarely signs of goodness" (*Analects* 1.3, 17.17). While Confucius believed that public image may have its place (*Analects* 12.2), he denounced one who merely "adopts the appearance of Goodness but violates it in his actual conduct" (*Analects* 12.20). Moreover, the ideal gentleman is the one who can live "free of anxiety and fear" because he can "look inside (himself) and find no faults" (*Analects* 12.4).

Like the *Analects*, the Sermon also calls for integrity (Matt 5:48).[97] Rather than focusing on externals, Jesus prioritized a disciple's private life (Matt 6:1–18) and the motivation (rather than the location) for doing good deeds.[98] Although good deeds are not to be hidden (Matt 5:14–16), public showiness can never replace personal piety.[99]

The *Analects* rightly point out the anxiety that arises from awareness of one's own faults. However, without a personal transcendent being, disciples are left to their own abilities to overcome their inadequacies. Jesus's answer to "anxiety and fear" due to personal failure (*Analects* 12.4) is rooted in a relationship with the heavenly Father who forgives sin and delivers from the evil one (Matt 6:12–14).[100] By reading the Sermon alongside the

---

97. Here, I follow Pennington, who argues that *teleios* in Matt 5:48 means "wholeness" or "integrity." Pennington, *Sermon on the Mount*, 69–85.

98. Quarles, *Sermon on the Mount*, 88.

99. Pennington, *Sermon on the Mount*, 163–64; Quarles, *Sermon on the Mount*, 86.

100. As Quarles, *Sermon on the Mount*, 31–34, argues, Jesus's entire sermon was predicated upon the new covenant where God replaces the disciple's sinful and rebellious heart of stone with a softened heart of flesh (Jer 31:33; Ezek 36:26). Moreover, in the new

"Your Heavenly Father Is Perfect"

*Analects*, we can better appreciate the personal heavenly Father who hears prayer (Matt 6:9), sees and rewards what is done in secret (Matt 6:4, 6, 18), and provides for our daily needs (Matt 6:25–34; 7:11).

## The Positive Use of Shame

Shame (恥 *chi*) is a broad topic in Confucian thought that could merit a separate essay. For brevity, I will cite just one example from the *Analects* that describes the positive use of shame for governing the masses:

> If you try to guide the common people with regulations and keep them in line with punishments, the common people will become evasive and will have no sense of shame. If, however, you guide them with Virtue, and keep them in line by means of ritual, the people will have a sense of shame and will rectify themselves. (*Analects* 2.3)

For Confucius, the ideal way to govern a society was to motivate them internally through the proper use of shame and ritual. Rather than relying solely on law and punishment, Confucius believed that shame was the key to a well-ordered society. While some cultures tend to view shame as a negative consequence for wrongdoing, the *Analects* suggest that shame can be used as a positive tool.[101] The positive role of shame in the *Analects* can provide fresh perspective for reading the Sermon with an eye toward the potential positive function of shame in Jesus's teaching.[102]

The Sermon's opening section, the Beatitudes, describes the "blessed" state of people whose lives are marked by lowliness and suffering.[103] Lowliness is exactly what the honor-seeking disciples did *not* want (Matt 18:1; 20:21).

---

covenant, God puts his own Holy Spirit within each believer to enable obedience and faith (Ezek 36:27). It is only through the new covenant that disciples can become whole persons rather than merely conforming externally.

101. In recent years, some works argue for the positive role of shame. See Lau, *Defending Shame*; Ten Elshof, *For Shame*.

102. Shame has different connotations in Chinese versus Western cultures. In this brief discussion of shame, I am unable to delve deeper into these differences. One recent work that discusses these differences is Chan, "Romans 8 and the Conception."

103. Neyrey, *Honor and Shame*, has shown various ways in which Matthew's Gospel depicts the dual themes of honor (whether ascribed or achieved) and shame. Examples of the honor theme include public declarations of Jesus's reputation (e.g., 2:1–4; 3:11–13, 17; 4:24–25; 7:28; 8:1; 9:26, 33; 11:2; 12:23; 13:2; 14:1, 34; 15:30–31; 16:13; 17:5; 19:1; 20:29; 21:9–11; 21:46; 22:33) and the disciples' desires for status (Matt 18:1–6; 19:13–15; 20:20–28).

However, in a series of dramatic reversals, the Beatitudes describe an upside-down world where the heavenly Father "honors the dishonored."[104] Although the disciples desired social status (Matt 18:1–6; 10:13–15; 20:20–28), Jesus declared that those who are shamed in this life will be rewarded in the next (cf. Matt 19:4; 20:26–27; 23:12).[105] Moreover, those who pursue public honor as a reward for their good works would receive no eternal reward. Instead, those who pursue true honor though private acts would be rewarded by the heavenly Father who sees what is done in secret (Matt 6:1–18).[106]

While the Beatitudes present the reversal of shame, the Sermon elsewhere uses shame to motivate virtuous behavior. On the day of judgment, those who say "Lord, Lord" (Matt 7:21) without a relationship with Christ will be publicly denounced and shamed (Matt 7:22–23). The judgment upon such a person represents a dramatic reversal compared to the earthly experience of ministering in Jesus's name (Matt 7:22).[107] In the Sermon's conclusion, those who refuse to obey Jesus's teaching are compared to a foolish builder whose house crumbles in a moment of shameful destruction (Matt 7:26).[108] It is fitting that Jesus would end his Sermon with a warning of impending shame and destruction to motivate the foolish person to obey his teaching.

## CONCLUSION

Confucius's *Analects* and Jesus's Sermon on the Mount undergird two major world philosophies that address common concerns surrounding the great questions of life.[109] Although separated by centuries, the two texts share remarkable similarities, such as their emphases on the importance of character, integrity, and the positive use of shame. While some (like Matteo Ricci)

---

104. Neyrey, *Honor and Shame*, 164–89.

105. Moreover, Jesus also provided the ultimate example by offering himself up as a ransom for many (Matt 20:28). Jesus would bear the humiliating shame of being mocked, flogged, and crucified before being raised back to glorious life on the third day (20:19).

106. Neyrey, *Honor and Shame*, 217.

107. Neyrey, *Honor and Shame*, 225–26. Their fate resembles that of the wedding guest who lacked wedding garments in Jesus's parable of the wedding banquet (Matt 22:1–14). Instead of being honored and considered worthy of invitation (22:8) he is cast out to a place of torment (22:13).

108. Neyrey, *Honor and Shame*, 226.

109. For example: What does a fulfilled life look like? What is the nature of right and wrong?

"Your Heavenly Father Is Perfect"

believed that Confucianism and Christianity were basically compatible, a closer look at the *Analects* and the Sermon reveal fundamental differences. Most notably, the ethics of the Sermon are based upon a personal transcendent heavenly Father who is both the model for (Matt 5:48) and rewarder of good deeds (Matt 6:4, 6, 18). The *Analects*, on the other hand, appeal to transcendent principles (e.g., *tian, li, dao*) but lack a personal transcendent being to motivate ethical behavior.

Reading the Sermon alongside the *Analects* can help readers appreciate the uniqueness of both works. A reader of the Sermon who is familiar with the *Analects* ought to have increased appreciation for the heavenly Father who listens to prayer and invites people to an intimate relationship with himself (Matt 7:11).[110] This is the same Father who calls believers to a high standard of integrity (Matt 5:48) and yet is quick to forgive when one's behavior falls short of his standards (Matt 6:12, 14–15). The heavenly Father provides for every need so that a disciple need not be anxious about life (Matt 6:26). The *Analects* help to draw our attention to ethical themes in the Sermon, such as (1) integrity and public image and (2) the positive use of shame. By providing an example of the positive role of shame for creating a well-ordered society, the *Analects* can be used as a helpful comparison for understanding the positive role of shame in the Sermon. Indeed, by reading the Sermon alongside the *Analects*, readers might better appreciate the Sermon's message and be better equipped to present its timeless message in dialogue with those from a Confucian background.

## BIBLIOGRAPHY

Barclay, John M. G. "'O wad some Pow'r the giftie gie us, To see oursels as others see us!': Method and Purpose in Comparing the New Testament." In *The New Testament in Comparison: Validity, Method and Purpose in Comparing Traditions*, edited by John M. G. Barclay and Benjamin G. White, 9–22. Library of New Testament Studies 600. London: T&T Clark, 2020.

Barclay, John M. G., and Benjamin G. White. "Introduction: Posing the Questions." In *The New Testament in Comparison: Validity, Method and Purpose in Comparing*

---

110. In the early years of Chinese Bible translation, the "term question" focused on the challenge of translating the word *God* into Chinese. Since the words available in Chinese already carried various connotations, disagreements among translators led to different terms being used in different versions of the Chinese Bible. While the question cannot be fully avoided, emphasizing God as the heavenly Father may be a fruitful strategy for presenting the Christian God using fresh categories to the Chinese. On the "term question" see Zetzsche, *Bible in China*, 82–90.

*Traditions*, edited by John M. G. Barclay and Benjamin G. White, 1–8. Library of New Testament Studies 600. London: T&T Clark, 2020.

Berthrong, John H. *All under Heaven: Transforming Paradigms in Confucian-Christian Dialogue*. SUNY Series in Chinese Philosophy and Culture. Albany, NY: State University of New York Press, 1994.

Chan, Yi-Sang Patrick. "Romans 8 and the Conception of Chinese Shame and Guilt." *Missio Dei: A Journal of Missional Theology and Praxis* 11 (2020). https://missiodeijournal.com/issues/md-11/authors/md-11-chan.

Chang, Lit-Sen. *Asia's Religions: Christianity's Momentous Encounter with Paganism*. Horizon Series. San Gabriel, CA: China Horizon, 1999.

Cua, Antonio S. "Confucianism: Ethics." In *Encyclopedia of Chinese Philosophy*, edited by Antonio S. Cua, 72–79. New York: Routledge, 2003.

Foster, Robert B. "Why on Earth Use 'Kingdom of Heaven'? Matthew's Terminology Revisited." *New Testament Studies* 48.4 (Oct. 2002) 487–99.

Gardner, Daniel K. *Confucianism: A Very Short Introduction*. Very Short Introductions 395. Oxford: Oxford University Press, 2014.

Goh, Elaine Wei-Fun. *Cross-Textual Reading of Ecclesiastes with the Analects: In Search of Political Wisdom in a Disordered World*. Contrapuntal Readings of the Bible in World Christianity 4. Eugene, OR: Pickwick, 2019.

Goldin, Paul Rakita. *Confucianism*. Ancient Philosophies. London: Routledge, 2014.

Hall, David L., and Roger T. Ames. *Thinking through Confucius*. SUNY Series in Systematic Philosophy. Albany, NY: State University of New York Press, 1987.

Huang, Paulos. *Confronting Confucian Understandings of the Christian Doctrine of Salvation: A Systematic Theological Analysis of the Basic Problems in the Confucian-Christian Dialogue*. Studies in Systematic Theology 3. Leiden: Brill, 2009.

Ivanhoe, Paul J. "Whose Confucius? Which Analects?" In *Confucius and the* Analects*: New Essays*, edited by Bryan W. Van Norden, 119–33. Oxford: Oxford University Press, 2002.

Lau, Te-Li. *Defending Shame: Its Formative Power in Paul's Letters*. Grand Rapids, MI: Baker Academic, 2020.

———. *The Politics of Peace: Ephesians, Dio Chrysostom, and the Confucian Four Books*. Supplements to Novum Testamentum 133. Leiden: Brill, 2010.

Lawrence, Arren Bennet. *Comparative Characterization in the Sermon on the Mount: Characterization of the Ideal Disciple*. Eugene, OR: Wipf & Stock, 2017.

Lee, Jung Young. *The Trinity in Asian Perspective*. Nashville: Abingdon, 1996.

Lewis, C. S. *Mere Christianity*. New York: HarperOne, 1952.

Lin, Yutang. *From Pagan to Christian*. Cleveland, OH: World Publishing, 1959.

Liu, Shu-hsien. "Li: Principle, Pattern, Reason." In *Encyclopedia of Chinese Philosophy*, edited by Antonio S. Cua, 364–70. New York: Routledge, 2003.

Longman, Tremper III. *The Fear of the Lord Is Wisdom: A Theological Introduction to Wisdom in Israel*. Grand Rapids, MI: Baker Academic, 2017.

Luz, Ulrich. *The Theology of the Gospel of Matthew*. Translated by J. Bradford Robinson. New Testament Theology. Cambridge, UK: Cambridge University Press, 1995.

Meynard, Thierry. *The Jesuit Reading of Confucius: The First Complete Translation of the* Lunyu *(1687) Published in the West*. Jesuit Studies 3. Leiden: Brill, 2015.

Neyrey, Jerome H. *Honor and Shame in the Gospel of Matthew*. Louisville, KY: Westminster John Knox, 1998.

## "Your Heavenly Father Is Perfect"

Ni, Peimin. *Understanding the* Analects *of Confucius: A New Translation of* Lunyu *with Annotations*. SUNY Series in Chinese Philosophy and Culture. Albany, NY: State University of New York Press, 2017.

Pennington, Jonathan T. *Heaven and Earth in the Gospel of Matthew*. Supplements to Novum Testamentum 126. Leiden: Brill, 2007.

———. *Jesus the Great Philosopher: Rediscovering the Wisdom Needed for the Good Life*. Grand Rapids, MI: Brazos, 2020.

———. *The Sermon on the Mount and Human Flourishing: A Theological Commentary*. Grand Rapids, MI: Baker Academic, 2017.

Puett, Michael. "Who Is Confucius in Today's China?" In *The China Questions: Critical Insights into a Rising Power*, edited by Jennifer M. Rudolph and Michael Szonyi, 231–36. Cambridge, MA: Harvard University Press, 2018.

Quarles, Charles L. *Sermon on the Mount: Restoring Christ's Message to the Modern Church*. New American Commentary Studies in Bible and Theology 11. Nashville: B&H Academic, 2011.

Richards, E. Randolph, and Brandon J. O'Brien. *Misreading Scripture with Western Eyes: Removing Cultural Blinders to Better Understand the Bible*. Downers Grove, IL: InterVarsity, 2012.

Roetz, Heiner. *Confucian Ethics of the Axial Age: A Reconstruction under the Aspect of the Breakthrough toward Postconventional Thinking*. SUNY Series in Chinese Philosophy and Culture. Albany, NY: State University of New York Press, 1993.

Rule, Paul A. "Jesuit and Confucian? Chinese Religion in the Journals of Matteo Ricci SJ 1583–1610." *Journal of Religious History* 5.2 (1968) 105–24.

Slingerland, Edward, trans. *Confucius* Analects*: With Selection from Traditional Commentaries*. Indianapolis: Hackett, 2003.

———. "The Situationist Critique and Early Confucian Virtue Ethics." *Ethics* 121.2 (2011) 390–419.

———. "Virtue Ethics, the 'Analects,' and the Problem of Commensurability." *Journal of Religious Ethics* 29.1 (2001) 97–125.

Smith, Jonathan Z. *Drudgery Divine: On the Comparison of Early Christianities and the Religions of Late Antiquity*. Chicago Studies in the History of Judaism. Chicago: University of Chicago Press, 1994.

Tang, Yijie. "Transcendence and Immanence in Confucian Philosophy." In *Confucian-Christian Encounters in Historical and Contemporary Perspective*, edited by Peter K. H. Lee., 171–81. Religions in Dialogue 5. Lewiston, NY: Edwin Mellen, 1991.

Ten Elshof, Gregg. *Confucius for Christians: What an Ancient Chinese Worldview Can Teach Us about Life in Christ*. Grand Rapids, MI: Eerdmans, 2015.

———. *For Shame: Rediscovering the Virtues of a Maligned Emotion*. Grand Rapids, MI: Zondervan, 2021.

Tennent, Timothy C. *Theology in the Context of World Christianity: How the Global Church Is Influencing the Way We Think about and Discuss Theology*. Grand Rapids, MI: Zondervan, 2007.

Thompson, Laurence G. *Chinese Religion: An Introduction*. 5th ed. Religious Life in History Series. Belmont, CA: Wadsworth, 1996.

Wilson, Stephen A. "Conformity, Individuality, and the Nature of Virtue: A Classical Confucian Contribution to Contemporary Ethical Reflection." *Journal of Religious Ethics* 23.2 (1995) 263–89.

## Integrating Theology, Church, and Ministry in a Chinese Seminary

Wright, Christopher J. H. *Old Testament Ethics for the People of God*. Downers Grove, IL: InterVarsity, 2004.

Yao, Xinzhong. *Confucianism and Christianity: A Comparative Study of Jen and Agape*. Brighton, UK: Sussex Academic Press, 1996.

———. *An Introduction to Confucianism*. New York: Cambridge University Press, 2000.

Yeo, Khiok-Khng. "The Logos and Pneuma of Creation: A Cross-Cultural Reading of Romans 8 and the Inspirited World." In *Spirit Wind: The Doctrine of the Holy Spirit in Global Theology—A Chinese Perspective*, edited by Peter L. H. Tie and Justin T. T. Tan, 147–61. Eugene, OR: Pickwick, 2021.

———. *What Has Jerusalem to Do with Beijing? Biblical Interpretation from a Chinese Perspective*. 2nd ed. Contrapuntal Readings of the Bible in World Christianity 2. Eugene, OR: Pickwick, 2018.

Yieh, John Y. H. "Reading the Sermon on the Mount in China: A Hermeneutical Enquiry into Its History of Reception." In *Reading Christian Scriptures in China*, edited by Chloë Starr, 143–62. T&T Clark Theology. London: T&T Clark, 2008.

Young, John D. *Confucianism and Christianity: The First Encounter*. Hong Kong: Hong Kong University Press, 1983.

Zetzsche, Jost Oliver. *The Bible in China: The History of the Union Version or the Culmination of Protestant Missionary Bible Translation in China*. Monumenta Serica Monograph Series 45. Nettetal, Ger.: Steyler, 1999.

Zhao, Yanxia. *Father and Son in Confucianism and Christianity: A Comparative Study of Xunzi and Paul*. Portland, OR: Sussex Academic Press, 2007.

# A Threefold Theological Interpretation and a Threefold Practical Implication of the "Spirit" (*pneuma*) in "The Spirit Is Willing, but the Flesh Is Weak" (Matt 26:41b)

Peter L. H. Tie

## INTRODUCTION

PETER AND THE OTHER disciples were determined to follow Jesus to the end, regardless of the cost. Peter replied to Jesus's forewarning of the disciples' desertion, "Even if all fall away on account of you, I never will" (Matt 26:33).[1] Jesus's reply to Peter's bold words seemed quite discouraging: "Truly I tell you . . . this very night, before the rooster crows, you will disown me three times" (26:34). No matter! Peter declared once more to seal his vow, and this time, he swore on his own life, "Even if I have to die with you, I will never disown you" (26:35a). Peter was not alone in this because "all the other disciples said the same" (26:35b). They were so eager to die for Jesus's cause, even though they might not have understood then what dying for Jesus actually meant.[2]

---

1. Unless stated otherwise, this writer uses New International Version (NIV 2011).
2. Hauerwas, *Matthew*, 221.

## Integrating Theology, Church, and Ministry in a Chinese Seminary

The disciples' commitment to follow Jesus and their readiness to give up their lives for Jesus were obvious. They were determined to do what was "right." Their emotions were so "fired up," like a manifestation of the lyrics to the hymn, "I have decided to follow Jesus. I have decided to follow Jesus . . . No turning back, no turning back." Ironically, when we turn our eyes to Jesus at that moment, he seemed very distressed and depressed "to the point of death" (26:37–38)—antithetical to the emotions of his disciples. Was it because Jesus knew he was about to die? If so, shouldn't Jesus have been a little excited or consoled by his disciples' radical willingness to die with him? Was it not what Jesus willed for his followers: "Whoever wants to be my disciple must deny themselves and take up their cross and follow me. For whoever wants to save their life will lose it, but whoever loses their life for me will find it" (16:24–25)? The next narrative leads us to the famous scene in the Garden of Gethsemane, where prayers happened (or did not happen), as well as where the wills of the disciples, the Son of Man, and the Father intersected (26:36–46).

The goal of this paper is to explore the possible meanings of the term *spirit* in Jesus's famous statement "The spirit [πνεῦμα; *pneuma*] is willing, but the flesh [σάρξ; *sarx*] is weak" (Matt 26:41b; parallel in Mark 14:38b).[3] This paper proposes a theological understanding of this *pneuma*. First, this writer will briefly review the classic "human spirit versus flesh" interpretation of the "spirit" in Jesus's statement based on five selected scholarly biblical commentaries. Then, the paper will focus on exploring the concept of *pneuma* (Matt 26:41b) from a threefold anthropological, pneumatological, and Christological standpoint, in accordance with the principle of the divine-human authorship and *sensus plenior* (literally, "fuller sense") of Scripture.[4] The aim of this new proposal is to demonstrate how this theological interpretation of *pneuma*, the "Spirit" (that is, the Holy Spirit) can better capture Jesus's statement of "the spirit is willing, but the flesh is weak" and shed light on practical implications.

### THE CLASSIC "HUMAN SPIRIT VERSUS FLESH" VIEW

Most biblical commentators argue that *pneuma* in Matt 26:41b refers to the "human spirit," which means a person's "heart," "intention," "attitude," etc.

---

3. Luke 22:39–46 also contains the Gethsemane event but does not have the statement "the spirit is willing, but the flesh is weak."

4. Tie, "Spirit, Scripture, Saints," 3–5, 14–19.

## A Threefold Theological Interpretation

(versus human "*sarx*, flesh, or body"). In a word, there is a spirit-flesh tension within a person. Here are five selected quotes attempting to interpret the "spirit" and "flesh" as referring to the disciples' (or human) condition at that time:

1. Craig Blomberg: "The human spirit has good intentions, but the *flesh* . . . is weak. Perhaps this saying of Jesus is one of the sources which provided Paul with his characteristic use of 'flesh.'"[5]

2. Grant R. Osborne: "The disciples want to obey Jesus and do what is right in the depths of their spirit, but their external flesh lacks the strength . . . . πρόθυμον [*prothymon*] means to be 'ready, eager, or desirous' to do something. It connotes good will and the willingness to do what God wants. So Jesus is saying that the disciples desire to stay awake and do what he is asking but lack the personal strength to do so."[6]

3. David L. Turner: "Their protests in 26:35b indicate their willingness of spirit (cf. Ps. 51:12), but their inability to remain alert with their master during his final and most difficult hours on earth reveals their weakness of flesh (Rom. 6:19; cf. 8:4–17; Gal. 5:16–24). . . . But spiritual alertness may overcome human weakness (cf. Rom. 13:11–14)."[7]

4. John Nolland: "'The spirit is willing,' is however, something that distinguishes the disciples from many others. They have been eager to identify themselves from Jesus and his project. They have recently declared their readiness to die for him [Matt 26:35]. . . . But for them too, there sits in the background the need, ultimately, to subject their wills to the divine will."[8]

5. Leon Morris: "Jesus recognizes that the disciples wanted to do as he has asked, but that they were not strong enough. Their physical bodies let them down. It has well been remarked that just at the time when Jesus was showing victory of spirit over flesh, the disciples were manifesting the victory of flesh over spirit . . . . Because of the frailty of human nature there is the constant need for prayer. A willing spirit is not enough; it must be supplemented by prevailing prayer."[9]

---

5. Blomberg, *Matthew*, 396.
6. Osborne, *Matthew*, 980–81.
7. Turner, *Matthew*, 632.
8. Nolland, *Gospel of Matthew*, 1102.
9. Morris, *Gospel according to Matthew*, 670.

Integrating Theology, Church, and Ministry in a Chinese Seminary

The aforementioned five commentators are sufficient to help us summarize "the spirit is willing (*prothymos*)" as the disciples' "willing attitude"; for example: "good intentions" (Blomberg); they "want to obey Jesus and do what is right in the depths of their spirit . . . good will and the willingness to do what God wants" (Osborne; also Morris); "willingness of spirit (cf. Ps. 51:12)" (Turner);[10] "eager[ness] to identify themselves from Jesus and his project . . . their readiness to die for him" (Nolland).

These commentators observe that there was a real struggle between a person's "spirit" and "flesh." The human "spirit" was usually deemed as a "stronger" element than one's weaker aspect, the "flesh" or "body." As Turner concludes in practical terms, "spiritual alertness may overcome human weakness." In general, despite the ambiguity of *sarx* (σὰρξ),[11] these commentators generally agree that the disciples were "willing" in "spirit"— eager to do what the Lord wanted—to die for the cause of Jesus (26:35b), but their "flesh" failed to sustain their willingness. Thus, Jesus stated the obvious and universal human condition as demonstrated by the disciples, "the spirit is willing, but the flesh is weak" (Matt 26:41b). Now, after reviewing the classic "human spirit versus flesh" view, we move on to the threefold theological interpretation.

---

10. Interestingly, this writer notes that the supposedly human "willing spirit" (πνεύματι ἡγεμονικῷ, *pneumati hēgemonikō*) in Ps 51:12 could refer to the "Holy Spirit" in the preceding verse (51:11): "Do not cast me from your presence or take your Holy Spirit from me. Restore to me the joy of your salvation and grant me a willing spirit, to sustain me." In fact, the *Greek-English Lexicon* suggests that the term ἡγεμονικός (*hēgemonikos*) has a sense of "being in a supervisory capacity, guiding, leading"; therefore, it can be translated as the "guiding Spirit," instead of "willing spirit" (Ps 51:12 ESV, NIV). Arndt et al., "Ἡγεμονικός," 433. See also Dahood, *Psalms II*, 7–8. This discussion is beyond the scope of this article.

11. Osborne takes σὰρξ (*sarx*) "flesh/body" to be "external flesh" representing human inability or vulnerability (Osborne, *Matthew*, 980–81). Morris is clearer in this aspect: σὰρξ (*sarx*) refers to "physical bodies"; "(frailty of) human nature" (Morris, *Gospel according to Matthew*, 670). Blomberg states that "flesh seems most likely to mean sinful human nature, though, in this case, including frail, physical weakness (a body that wants to sleep) as well" (Blomberg, *Matthew*, 396).

A Threefold Theological Interpretation

# A THREEFOLD THEOLOGICAL INTERPRETATION: ANTHROPOLOGICAL, PNEUMATOLOGICAL, AND CHRISTOLOGICAL

## Anthropological Perspective

The essential question for our discussion is: Does the "spirit" (*pneuma*) here in Matt 26:41b refer to the human "spirit" in conflict with one's own "flesh," that is, a "spirit versus flesh dichotomy"? In order to answer this question, we need to have a closer look at Matthew, the rest of the Gospels, and even other New Testament writings (esp. Rom 7) for clues. My initial investigation indicates that the Gospel authors and Paul hardly reveal a human "spirit versus flesh" conflict.

Matthew 10:28 may suggest a dichotomy of human nature: "Do not be afraid of those who kill the body [σῶμα, *sōma*] but cannot kill the soul [ψυχή, *psychē*]. Rather, be afraid of the One who can destroy both soul [ψυχή] and body [σῶμα] in hell" (Matt 10:28). However, this verse does not help with interpreting Matt 26:41b, because: (1) the former used ψυχή (*psychē*) and σῶμα (*sōma*), rather than πνεῦμα (*pneuma*) and σάρξ (*sarx*), although the words are actually interchangeable or synonymous in certain cases; (2) Matt 10:28 speaks more of the unity of soul and body, rather than the tension between the soul and body of a person.

Another possible instance that shows the spirit versus flesh dichotomy is John 6:63: "The Spirit gives life; the flesh counts for nothing. The words I have spoken to you—they are full of the Spirit and life." Osborne observed that, in the four Gospels, John 6:63 is the only instance (other than Matt 26:41b; parallel in Mark 14:38b) that shows the "spirit versus flesh dichotomy."[12] If, however, Osborne took this "spirit" (in John 6:63) to mean the "human spirit," this would suggest that "the human spirit gives oneself life." In the context of John 6, this could imply that "human spirit" is able to provide "eternal life." Such an interpretation would be doctrinally disastrous. While he did not specifically identify the "spirit" in Matt 26:41b with human spirit, Osborne *did* immediately connect the concept of "spirit versus flesh dichotomy" to Paul's teaching on the Holy Spirit and human flesh in Rom 8: "This [Matt 26:41b and Mark 14:38b] and John 6:63 are the only instances of spirit vs. flesh dichotomy in the Gospels, but it is developed further in Paul, who uses 'spirit' (πνεῦμα; *pneuma*) for the Holy

---

12. Osborne, *Matthew*, 980.

Spirit in Romans 8, thereby contrasting life in the Spirit with life in one's own strength."[13] In a word, Osborne did not give a clear conclusion that the "spirit" in Matt 26:41b refers to the human spirit or the Holy Spirit.[14]

One may assume that the classic "spirit-flesh" view may use Rom 7 as a crucial place to argue for its position. It is, however, interesting to note that none of the aforementioned five NT scholars link Matt 26:41b to Rom 7 where Paul clearly stated his inner struggle, "I do not understand what I do. For what I want to do I do not do, but what I hate I do.... For I have the desire to do what is good, but I cannot carry it out. For I do not do the good I want to do, but the evil I do not want to do—this I keep on doing" (Rom 7:15, 18b–19). One of the possible reasons for the lack of such a link is that, although there is frequent mention of human *sarx* (flesh) in 7:5, 18, 25, Paul did not use the word *pneuma* to refer to human "spirit" in Rom 7, except 7:6, where it most likely refers to the Holy Spirit. So, there is no clear case of the "spirit versus flesh" dichotomy in Rom 7. Fee states emphatically, "Whatever else, this passage [Rom 7] does *not* describe a struggle within the believer between his or her flesh and the Spirit, but rather describes what it is like to be under the law while in the clutches of sin and the flesh."[15] Paul's argument for his personal inner conflict is based on the reality of "sinful nature" (Rom 7:17b, 20b), that one is morally unable to achieve the standard of God's law (Rom 7:14).[16] More importantly, Paul's continuous argument in Rom 8 (see following sections) demonstrates that it is essentially not a struggle between a person's own "spirit and flesh," but an ongoing battle between the "desire of the [Holy] Spirit" and the "desire of the [human] flesh" (e.g., Rom 8:5–6, 9–13).[17]

From an anthropological standpoint, there is no clue to be found from the Gospel writers (or Paul) to help us determine whether the "spirit" in Matt 26:41b is human or divine, in conflict with one's "flesh." The next

---

13. Osborne, *Matthew*, 980.

14. Matthew 5:3 "poor in spirit" (taken to mean one's "attitude or state of mind") and Matt 27:50 "gave up his spirit" (taken to mean Jesus's life force). Nolland deemed these two instances to be unhelpful for interpreting the "spirit" in Matt 26:41b (Nolland, *Gospel of Matthew*, 1100n187).

15. Fee, *God's Empowering Presence*, 513. Emphasis original.

16. Kruse, *Paul's Letter to the Romans*, 305–8.

17. NT scholars consider Rom 6:1—8:39 as a distinct literary unit, so it is adequate to explain Paul's internal struggle in Rom 7 in light of its immediate and relevant context (i.e., Rom 8). Fee, *God's Empowering Presence*, 499, 514–15.

## A Threefold Theological Interpretation

section will attempt to interpret the "spirit" in Matt 26:41b from a pneumatological perspective, especially in light of Paul's writings in Rom 8 and Gal 5.

### Pneumatological Perspective

Nolland recognizes the difficulty of identifying the meaning of "spirit" in Matt 26:41b. It could mean the "life force" or "various kinds of aptitudes and attitudes" as in the OT, or two opposing spirits (or impulses) within a human person, an idea found in the Qumran.[18] Some may suggest that Jesus's statement "the spirit is willing, but the flesh is weak" could be the basis on which Paul developed his "Spirit versus flesh" theology.[19] We will comment briefly on the relevant passages of Paul's "Spirit versus flesh" struggle in Rom 8 and Gal 5, against the backdrop of Matt 26:41b.

On Rom 8:1–17, Schreiner rightly comments: Christians "are no longer in the flesh, but in the *Spirit*. The natural proclivity of the flesh is to think on the things of the flesh and to carry out its desires. Similarly, those who have the Spirit do what the Spirit desires. Paul is aware of the tension between the already and not yet; thus he reminds believers that the resurrection of the body is still future (8:10–11)."[20] Perhaps one could argue that Paul's use of "Spirit" (*pneuma*) versus "flesh" (*sarx*) was "developed" from Matt 26:41b (or Mark 14:38b). Nevertheless, Paul's use of them is quite clear that, in the "Spirit versus flesh dichotomy," *pneuma* (πνεῦμα) refers to the Holy Spirit. For *sarx* (σάρξ), it seems to have a double meaning, one referring to some kind of evil force that enslaves and entices, and the other referring to human "flesh"—the sinful condition of human nature (including one's physical body and soul/spirit). Nolland observes the difference between Matthew and Paul: "Paul goes a step further and can identify 'flesh'

---

18. Nolland, *Gospel of Matthew*, 1102.

19. Blomberg, *Matthew*, 396. Blomberg only suggests a connection/development of the "flesh" between Matt 26:41b and Paul: "Perhaps this saying of Jesus is one of the sources which provided Paul with his characteristic use of 'flesh,'" but does not suggest any connection of the "spirit and flesh" struggle between Matt 26:41b and Paul's writings (e.g., Rom 8 and Gal 5).

20. Schreiner, *Romans*, 393. Emphasis added. When contrasting the "body" (σῶμα, *sōma*) and the "spirit" (πνεῦμα, *pneuma*) in Rom 8:10, the latter could be referring to the Holy Spirit, instead of the human "spirit": "But if Christ is in you, although the body is dead because of sin, the Spirit is life because of righteousness" (ESV); "the Spirit gives life because of righteousness" (CSB).

as an evil power working through the appetites and wishes of the human frame. 'Flesh' in Mt. 26:41 is not like Paul's use (if it were, the difficulty would be caused by the flesh being strong, not weak)."[21] Nolland would definitely agree with the other meaning of "flesh" in Paul's writing, namely, the sinful state of human nature.[22] In this latter meaning, the "flesh" can be considered as "weak," that is, the inability to fulfill the law or the will of God (Rom 8:3). The "flesh" as "weak" is consistent with Matt 26:41b's "the flesh is weak" (ἡ δὲ σὰρξ ἀσθενής) and Rom 8:3's "it was weakened by the flesh" (ἠσθένει διὰ τῆς σαρκός). If it is so, how do we perceive a close connection between Matthew and Paul with regard to πνεῦμα (pneuma)?

For Paul, there is a constant struggle between the human "flesh" and divine "Spirit." As aforementioned, however, biblical scholars often cite Matt 26:41b as the foundation for Paul's Spirit versus flesh theology. If that is the case, they have to consider the radical shift from the human spirit versus flesh to the Holy Spirit versus flesh. Nolland correctly observes that "Paul has nothing comparable. Over against Paul's distinctive use of 'flesh' is to be set 'the Holy Spirit' (e.g., Rom. 8:9). Where are we to locate Mt. 26:41?"[23]

Paul's teaching in Gal 5:16–18 also does not show any hint of the inner struggle of human spirit versus flesh, but the passage does demonstrate divine Spirit versus human flesh.[24] Longenecker's interpretation of the same passage sufficiently captures the essence of Paul's argument:

> Yet behind the individual believer Paul sees two ethical forces that seek to control a person's thought and activity: the one, the personal Spirit of God; the other, the personified "flesh." . . . "[T]he flesh" and "the Spirit" are diametrically opposed to one another, with the result that one cannot do what he or she knows to be right when in "the flesh" (i.e., when living only humanly according to one's own guidance and the direction of whatever is simply human) but only when in "the Spirit" (i.e., when living in the new reality of being "in Christ" and directed by God's Spirit).[25]

21. Nolland, *Gospel of Matthew*, 1102.

22. Schreiner interprets the "flesh" (in Rom 8:3a) as "unregenerate human beings" (Schreiner, *Romans*, 394).

23. Nolland, *Gospel of Matthew*, 1102.

24. For context, "But I say, walk by the Spirit, and you will not carry out the desire of the flesh. For the desire of the flesh is against the Spirit, and the Spirit against the flesh; for these are in opposition to one another, in order to keep you from doing whatever you want. But if you are led by the Spirit, you are not under the Law" (Gal 5:16–18 NASB).

25. Longenecker, *Galatians*, 245.

## A Threefold Theological Interpretation

Paul's use of Holy Spirit versus human flesh is consistent in both Gal 5 and Rom 8; therefore, one may conclude that Matthew's human spirit versus flesh condition finds no correspondence in Paul's teaching on Spirit versus flesh. Subsequently, one has to deal with this significant question: Is there a "disunity" between the Gospel writers and Paul with regard to the view of the "s/Spirit versus flesh" tension?

Matthew's *pneuma* (Matt 26:41b), as most commentators have stated, likely refers to the human "spirit" (state of mind) which was "willing" and "eager," and had a "desire to do." It has been traditionally interpreted that the disciples were willing to die for Jesus, but they were too tired and weak to pray (as 26:43b notes, "because their eyes were heavy"). One may also put it this way: the disciples' "spirit is willing [to pray], but the flesh is weak [to pray]." Even though they *knew* praying was the "right" thing to do, they did not do it because of their physical fatigue.[26] Was it really the physical tiredness that defeated their spirit's willingness, resulting in their prayerlessness? Was it really a personal or internal struggle that the human "spirit" was "willing" but the human "flesh" was "weak"? It might be true that they were physically weak at the time, but they used to fish all night without sleep (Luke 5:5). We can understand that the disciples had to work through the night because their livelihood depended on the catch. On another occasion, even in the midst of a sea storm at night (Mark 4:35), they were not tired at all, but, ironically, Jesus turned in early. They had to wake Jesus up because their life depended on him.

One may reasonably deduce that it was not so much about the physical strength, but more about the heart's "willingness," "eagerness," or "desire" that motivates one's physical body to act. For example, some of us can stay up all night if the goal is to finish research papers, watch movies, play video games, care for a dying person in the hospital, or earn a living—whatever we really want (desire and passion) or actually have to accomplish (need or obligation). We may be physically weak but our sense of "willingness," "desire," "need," or "responsibility" compels us to persevere. So, concerning the disciples' "sleepy" condition, I suspect that it was not so much the "weak physical body" but the "*un*willing spirit" (or, at least, not willing enough to pray) that provides another more plausible explanation for the disciples' prayerlessness or sleepiness than the apparent cause of

---

26. GOD'S WORD® translation conveys this exact meaning: "You want to do what's right, but you're weak."

physical tiredness, that is, "heavy eyes" (Matt 26:43) or "exhaust[ion] from sorrow" (Luke 22:45).

In the context of Matt 26:41, the disciples were so "eager" or "willing" to die for the cause of Christ (Matt 26:33, 35), but at the same time, they refused to trust Jesus's words (prophecy) about their "falling away" (Matt 26:31, 34). If we interpret "the spirit is willing" as the disciples' (esp. Peter's) "willingness" to follow Christ even to death, their willingness, obviously, was a kind of self-confident human "desire" or "passion" that neglected/distrusted the words of Jesus. This kind of passion corresponds with what Longenecker explains about Paul's teaching on the "flesh," that is, "when living only humanly according to one's own guidance and the direction of whatever is simply human."[27] Their willingness seemed to be self-directed, rather than Spirit-guided. From this perspective, if we interpret "the spirit is willing" to mean only the disciples' "eagerness" or "desire to do something" or "knowing the right thing to do," their willingness is actually self-directed will; it is, in fact, "in the flesh," not "in the Spirit," according to Paul's "Spirit versus flesh" perspective. If only they had been more "willing" to believe in Jesus's words about their impending "fall" in the first place, they would have been more "willing" to pray, as Jesus commanded (Matt 26:41). In other words, if the *pneuma* in Matt 26:41b refers to the "spirit" of the disciples, then the phrase "the spirit is willing" has a negative connotation, that is, the disciples' willingness of spirit actually fell short, becoming self-directed and insufficient. In this sense, both their "spirit" and "flesh" were "weak."

Let us continue to consider the statement "the spirit is willing, but flesh is weak" from Jesus's own manner of prayer (a Christological perspective) to assess further which interpretation is more plausible: the traditional meaning of the human "spirit versus flesh" or the theological interpretation of "divine Spirit versus human flesh."

## Christological Perspective

Jesus himself showed obvious weakness of his "flesh" through his manner, which is a visible expression of his emotions:

- "He began to be sorrowful and troubled" (Matt 26:37).
- "My soul [*psychē*] is overwhelmed with sorrow to the point of death" (Matt 26:38a).

27. Longenecker, *Galatians*, 245.

## A Threefold Theological Interpretation

Compared to his disciples, Jesus seemed much less "willing" to die and expressed many more "fleshly" emotions (e.g., sorrow, grief, anxiety, and/or distress), suggesting he was very "unwilling," and his "flesh" was extremely "weak" (cf. Luke 22:44). Was Jesus so "weak" in his "soul"[28] that he expressed "human" emotions of distress and anxiety (Matt 26:38)? Morris observed that, ultimately, "when Jesus was showing the victory of spirit over flesh, the disciples were manifesting the victory of flesh over spirit."[29] Morris's conclusion is indicative of a "spirit versus flesh" dichotomy. This implies again that one's "spirit" is "stronger" than the "flesh," and the victory seems to rely on one's "spirit." If my earlier assessment is correct, the disciples' "willingness" in "spirit" was, in fact, insufficient, conceited, and self-directed (that is, in Paul's language, more "in the flesh").

The biblical doctrine of sin, however, teaches that each human person is fully depraved by sin. Nonetheless, many often apply the notion of the "sinful state of human nature" to human "flesh-body," which seemingly does not include the sinfulness of one's "spirit." We often talk about the frailty of physical "flesh," as if it is the main locus in which Satan tempts, rather than the human spirit or heart as the cause of sinfulness. Unfortunately, this negligence of the "sinful spirit" contributes to the dichotomic perspective of human spirit versus flesh, such as Morris's concept of the victory of one's "spirit over flesh."[30]

---

28. The word *psychē* (usually translated as "soul") and *pneuma* (usually translated as "spirit") are distinguishable in definitions, but also interchangeable in certain instances. For example, Matthew quoted the prophet Isaiah, "Behold, my servant whom I have chosen, my beloved with whom my soul [ψυχή, *psychē*] is well pleased" (Matt 12:18a ESV). One truly misses the point if he/she interprets literally that God has a "soul." The term *soul* is used by Yahweh, most likely referring to God's love toward Christ. As indicated in other Gospels, Jesus's emotions are also related to his "spirit" (πνεῦμα, *pneuma*), not just his "soul": Jesus "sighed deeply in his spirit" (Mark 8:12a ESV); "Jesus was troubled in his spirit" (John 13:21a ESV). These few examples demonstrate that: (1) We should not "sanctify" the word *soul* to restrict it to a single meaning; (2) we should not simply assume that the word *soul* always means "human soul" because doing so neglects the fact that the term *soul* can be used for God as well, and even more so for Jesus, the God-man; (3) we should not be tempted to interpret Jesus's emotions in his "soul" to relate it to his humanity, therefore disconnecting it/them from his divine nature. God has and shows emotions, too. In fact, both God and man have emotions; in other words, having emotions is part of being created in God's image. On God's emotions, see Lamb, *Emotions of God*, 1–22 ("Emotions Are Divine").

29. Morris, *Gospel according to Matthew*, 670.

30. Morris takes "flesh" to mean "physical bodies" and/or "human nature." Morris, *Gospel according to Matthew*, 670.

## Integrating Theology, Church, and Ministry in a Chinese Seminary

Many Christian doctrines perceive a human being as a whole (in two distinct aspects of spirit and body, and yet in one whole person). The doctrine of sin holds that the whole person is depraved by sin, including one's body and spirit.[31] The doctrine of incarnation and salvation teaches that Jesus took on the whole human nature, including both human body and spirit, in order to redeem the whole human. The doctrine of sanctification is about yielding our whole person—body and spirit—to the Holy Spirit in order to yield the fruit of the Spirit (Gal 5:16–25).[32] The doctrine of resurrection points to a future reality of the spirit and body becoming whole again, transformed to enjoy eternal bliss. From initial sinfulness to ultimate glorification, there is no apparent human spirit versus flesh conflict, but there is the constant struggle between the Holy Spirit and the human "flesh" (that is, the whole person—both spirit and body), which is distorted by sin and inclined to do according to one's desire instead of the Holy Spirit's desire. Instead of focusing on the internal struggle of a person, between one's flesh and one's spirit, the central idea of the spiritual struggle is whether the person is willing to obey the desire of the Holy Spirit (that is, God's will).

A case in point, Adam and Eve's fall into temptation was not simply due to their physical desires (in terms of taste and sight, Gen 3:6a),[33] but their "spiritual" or willful desire (i.e., desire for God's knowledge, Gen 3:6b) to directly disobey God's will and word (Gen 2:16–17). In the NT, Matthew (and Jesus) also recognized the "heart" as the origin of human sinfulness (Matt 15:18–19), not the physical flesh. Gordon Fee emphatically states, "It would be unthinkable to the Hebrew that sin lay in the flesh, since sin's origins lie in the human heart."[34] In other words, the "spirit versus flesh" dichotomy, or Jesus's overcoming his "flesh" with his "spirit," may not be the best (or only) way to understand "the spirit is willing, but the flesh is weak."

Prayer is the focus here in relation to the *pneuma* and the *sarx*: "Watch and pray so that you will not fall into temptation. The spirit is willing, but the flesh is weak" (Matt 26:41). Jesus's own persistence in prayer reveals

---

31. Nolland, *Gospel of Matthew*, 1102.

32. John pointed out the reality of Christians who may sin occasionally and the truth of Christ's perpetual forgiveness for those who approach him with true repentance (1 John 1:9; 2:1–2).

33. The statement "When the woman saw that the fruit of the tree was good for food and pleasing to the eye, and also desirable for gaining wisdom, she took some and ate it" corresponds with 1 John 2:16, "For everything in the world—the lust of the flesh, the lust of the eyes, and the pride of life—comes not from the Father but from the world."

34. Fee, *Paul, the Spirit*, 129.

## A Threefold Theological Interpretation

the will (desire) of the Father, as well as his own will (desire) to follow the Father's plan:

- "My Father, if it is possible, may this cup be taken from me. Yet not as I will, but as you will" (26:39b).[35]
- "He went away a second time and prayed, 'My Father, if it is not possible for this cup to be taken away unless I drink it, may your will be done'" (26:42).
- "[Jesus] prayed the third time, saying the same thing" (26:44b).

Unlike Jesus, the disciples seemed to have no "willingness," "eagerness," or "desire" to pray. Perhaps they did not sense the urgent need to do so, even though they most likely knew that it was the "right" thing to do. Jesus, on the other hand, did not show any tension between his own "spirit" and his "flesh" (he seemed to be "weak" in both). Instead, it was more a "struggle" between his desire (will) and the Father's desire (will), a condition that is more aligned with Paul's words in Rom 8:5–6 about the struggle between whether to follow the desire of the Spirit (what God wants) or the desire of the "flesh" (what a person wants). Paul further connected his "Spirit versus flesh" concept with the Spirit's intercession (or praying) in human weakness: "In the same way, the Spirit helps us in our weakness. We do not know what we ought to pray for, but the Spirit himself intercedes for us through wordless groans. And he who searches our hearts knows the mind of the Spirit, because the Spirit intercedes for God's people in accordance with the will of God" (Rom 8:26–27).

In light of Paul's teaching, perhaps we may argue that when Jesus uttered "the Spirit is willing, but the flesh is weak," he was revealing a wonderful truth (as a promise) that even though the disciples were "weak in flesh," the Holy Spirit was always "willing," indicating the Spirit's will of praying for them in spite of their weakness. The Spirit's "willing" work in prayer during the disciples' "weakness" (Matt 26:41b) might have been further developed by Paul: The Holy Spirit "helps" in believers' "weakness" by constantly praying for them according to the Father's will, despite their ignorance of God's will, which is reflected in the deficiency of their prayers (Rom 8:26–27).[36]

---

35. NRSV (1989) uses one's desire ("want"), rather than one's mind ("will"): "My Father, if it is possible, let this cup pass from me; yet not what I want but what you want" (Matt 26:39b).

36. Schreiner, *Romans*, 434–39.

# Integrating Theology, Church, and Ministry in a Chinese Seminary

## A THREEFOLD PRACTICAL IMPLICATION

After a brief investigation of the classic human "spirit versus flesh" view and a theological interpretation of *pneuma* (Matt 26:41b) from an anthropological-pneumatological-Christological perspective, this writer concludes:

- Since there is no clear biblical correspondence to the human "spirit versus flesh" struggle but only the unity of human spirit and body in the four Gospels;

- since there is no direct human "spirit versus flesh" but only the Holy "Spirit versus flesh" conflict in Paul's writings (esp. Rom 8 and Gal 5);

- since there is no evident struggle between the "spirit" and "flesh" of Jesus, but only between the wills of Jesus and the Father;

- since there is no Christian doctrine that directly supports the human "spirit versus flesh" struggle;

- therefore, the "*pneuma*" in Matt 26:41b is better taken to mean the "Holy Spirit," instead of the human "spirit."

Subsequently, the threefold practical implication of taking *pneuma* in Matt 26:41b to be the Holy Spirit is as follows:[37]

*Promise of the Spirit, rather than the conflict within human nature.* If it is true that Matt 26:41b refers to the Holy Spirit, this indicates that Jesus revealed the promise of the Spirit's active work despite human weaknesses. However, if the "spirit is willing" refers to a person's natural and fallen condition—that is, one's eagerness to do a certain thing but inability to do it—this is a condition that anyone already knows through personal experience or general revelation.[38] For example, there is an idiom from Confucian *Analects*: "心有餘, 力不足," literally translated as "the will is there, but not the strength."[39] In most cases, this human "spirit as willing, strength as weak" results in inaction, or it becomes an excuse for not being able to do anything,

---

37. The Aramaic Bible in Plain English unambiguously uses "Spirit" in Matt 26:41b: "The Spirit is ready, but the body is weak."

38. Kruse provides a list of extrabiblical examples that show the common knowledge of "classical authors that appear similar to Paul's depiction of humanity's inability to perform the good they want to do and to desist from the evil they do not want to do [in Rom 7]." Kruse, *Paul's Letter to the Romans*, 312–13.

39. Or "I really want to do it, but don't have the resources." See Linguee.com, "心有餘而力不足—English Translation." As noted, the translation tool also uses "the spirit is willing but the flesh is weak" as one of the translation options for the Chinese idiom.

## A Threefold Theological Interpretation

due to either lack of strength or other resources. Nevertheless, when we understand *pneuma* in Matt 26:41b to be God's Spirit, this gives us great comfort and assurance that it is essentially God's Spirit whose constant will or work operates through his people, even in their fear or weakness (see Phil 2:12–13).[40] The Spirit can work *through* our weaknesses *in spite of* our prayerlessness.[41] This concept should not be an excuse for believers' prayerlessness, but a reminder of the wonderful promise of the Spirit's faithfulness in praying for believers, independent of their weaknesses.

*Prayer as the Spirit's work, regardless of human weakness.* Jesus's words urging his disciples to "watch and pray so that you will not fall into temptation" (Matt 26:41a) provide the context for Matt 26:41b. If the *pneuma* in Matt 26:41b refers to the divine Spirit, we may interpret the verse to mean that "the Spirit is willing [to pray], but the flesh is weak [to pray]." It is, then, not primarily about the disciples' readiness to die for Jesus's cause or their knowing of the right thing to do and not doing it, but rather the "readiness" of the Spirit of God to pray for the disciples, even when they were too "weak" to pray. The Spirit's intercession for the disciples, though implied in Matt 26:41b, must have laid the foundation for Paul's explicit teaching on the Spirit's intercession for believers (Rom 8:26–27).

Schreiner argues that, in Rom 8:26, the believers' "weakness" specifically refers to the "content" (not the "manner") of believers' prayers, because "they do not have an adequate grasp of what God's will is when they pray. Because of our finiteness and fallibility, we cannot fully perceive what God would desire."[42] While Schreiner is correct to note that Paul emphasized the "content" of believers' prayers, Matthew's account of Jesus's prayers in Gethsemane demonstrated that Jesus prayed "concise" prayers

---

40. While the Greek adjective *prothymos* ("willing, ready," as in Matt 26:41b) normally refers to human "willingness" (e.g., 1 Chr 28:21; 2 Chr 29:31; Hab 1:8; 2 Macc 4:14; 15:9; 3 Macc 5:26), it can be applied to God in the form of God's "readiness to bless." For example: "they are to bear on their forehead and their arm those wonders which declare the power of God, and his good will towards them, that God's readiness to bless them [τὸ περὶ αὐτοὺς πρόθυμον τοῦ θεοῦ, literally: the will of God concerning them] may appear everywhere conspicuous about them." Josephus, *Works of Josephus*, 117 (in "Antiquities of the Jews," bk. 4, 8.13; or 4:213).

41. On Rom 8:27, Schreiner states, "Believers, then, should take tremendous encouragement that the will of God is being fulfilled in their lives despite their weakness and inability to know what to pray for. God's will is not frustrated because of the weakness of believers. It is being fulfilled because the Spirit intercedes for us and invariably receives affirmative answers to his pleas." Schreiner, *Romans*, 439.

42. Schreiner, *Romans*, 435.

repeatedly and passionately (Matt 26:39, 42, 44); this posture indicates that, sometimes, the "manner" of prayers is as important as the "content" of prayers. Furthermore, no human (neither the disciples then nor believers now) can grasp God's will fully, but this does not mean prayers are never needed. It is precisely because of human "finiteness and fallibility" that believers must pray to gradually draw closer to God's will, rather than wait to fully grasp God's will before offering any prayers. The disciples might not have fully grasped the whole will of God, but they did have at least one clear "will" of the Lord, that is, to "watch and pray" (Matt 26:41). Believers' prayers signify their total dependence on the Holy Spirit, whereas the Spirit's prayers for the believers are totally independent of their finitude.

The Spirit's intercession for believers is a theological concept that appears nowhere else in the Bible, except in Rom 8, and now also in Matt 26:41b (and its Markan parallel), though only briefly. By placing Matt 26:41b and Rom 8:26–27 side by side, my proposal for Jesus's statement in Gethsemane is: The Holy Spirit is willing to pray for the disciples according to God's will, even though the human flesh is too "weak" to pray. Even when God's people are prone to follow the "flesh" ("what humans desire"), that is, not wanting to pray (manner of heart) or not knowing what to pray for (content of prayer), the Holy Spirit is always ready to pray for them ("what the Spirit desires") according to God's will. "Willingness to pray" (manner) and "prayer according to God's will" (content) are the constant works of the Spirit who indwells believers (cf. Rom 8:9–11).

*Purpose of prayers, where believers are called to participate in the trinitarian communication.* While Jesus was weak in "flesh," his persistent prayers to his Father ("not as I will, but as you will") and his statement ("the Spirit is willing" [to pray according to God's will]) reveal God's mysterious trinitarian relationship, where the wills of the Father, the Son, and the Spirit are not three separate wills but one united will.[43] Although believers are unable to perceive the whole will of God perfectly and, therefore, do not always get their prayers answered, the work of intercession according to God's will primarily belongs to the trinitarian work of the Son (Rom 8:34; Heb 7:25; 1 John 2:1) in the Spirit (Rom 8:26–27) to the Father. In a sense, Jesus's call for his disciples to pray is a gracious call to participate in the inner-trinitarian

---

43. If the *pneuma* (in Matt 26:41b) refers to the Holy Spirit, then the scene of prayer in Gethsemane adds to Matthew's other explicit trinitarian passages that show the presence of the Father, Son, and Spirit (e.g., Jesus's conception in Matt 1:20–23; baptism in 3:16–17; sending in 10:19–23; fulfillment in 12:17–18; identity in 22:41–45; temptation in 4:1–11; commission in 28:19–20). Wenk, "Holy Spirit," 391.

## A Threefold Theological Interpretation

communication. Prayer is, therefore, not a duty, but a privilege. Prayer is not of human effort, but of the Trinity's work. Prayer is the wonderful and mysterious wisdom of God's plan to lead the disciples (and us today) away from temptations (i.e., rejecting God's will), and to grow their and our obedience into God's desire (or will), as Jesus demonstrated in his prayers.

Jesus himself kept returning to prayer; his persistence showed his "willingness" to pray, surely being prompted by the "willing" Spirit, in a way that conforms to the Father's will, despite Jesus's "weakness" in his whole person, soul/spirit and flesh (Matt 26:37–38).[44] Jesus uttered similar (and perhaps, concise) prayers three times, but his prayers revealed that his seemingly "unwilling" desire was growing closer or obediently to the desire of God the Father. In a similar vein, however "weak" they may be, the believers' ongoing obedience in prayers guided by the Spirit through the Son will be ultimately in line with the Father's will, rather than bowing to the temptation of rejecting God's desire. May the Holy Spirit prompt, guide, and teach us to pray, in spite of our weakness.

## BIBLIOGRAPHY

Arndt, William F., et al. "Ἡγεμονικός." In *A Greek-English Lexicon of the New Testament and Other Early Christian Literature*, edited by Frederick W. Danker, 433. Logos Software. Chicago: University of Chicago Press, 2000.

Berkouwer, G. C. *Man: The Image of God*. Studies in Dogmatics. Grand Rapids, MI: Eerdmans, 1962.

Blomberg, Craig L. *Matthew*. New American Commentary 22. Nashville: Broadman, 1992.

Cooper, John W. "Scripture and Philosophy on the Unity of Body and Soul: An Integrative Method for Theological Anthropology." In *The Ashgate Research Companion to Theological Anthropology*, edited by Joshua R. Farris and Charles Taliaferro, 27–42. New York: Routledge, 2015.

Dahood, Mitchell. *Psalms II: 51–100*. 3rd ed. Anchor Bible Series 17. Garden City, NY: Doubleday, 1968.

Erickson, Millard J. *Christian Theology*. 3rd ed. Grand Rapids, MI: Baker Academic, 2013.

Fee, Gordon D. *God's Empowering Presence: The Holy Spirit in the Letters of Paul*. Peabody, MA: Hendrickson, 1994.

———. *Paul, the Spirit, and the People of God*. Peabody, MA: Hendrickson, 1996.

---

44. See Ps 51:10–12 (ESV): "Create in me a clean heart, O God, and renew a right spirit within me. Cast me not away from your presence, and take not your Holy Spirit from me. Restore to me the joy of your salvation, and uphold me with a willing spirit." David's psalm reveals his prayer to God for the Holy Spirit to restore in him a "willing spirit" (51:12), or "a right spirit" (51:10). Based on footnotes 10 and 40 of this chapter, it is reasonable to argue that the human's "willing spirit" is entirely dependent on the "willing Spirit."

Hauerwas, Stanley. *Matthew*. Brazos Theological Commentary on the Bible. Grand Rapids, MI: Brazos, 2006.
Josephus, Flavius. *The Works of Josephus: Complete and Unabridged*. Translated by William Whiston. Updated ed. Logos Software. Peabody, MA: Hendrickson, 1987.
Kruse, Colin G. *Paul's Letter to the Romans*. Pillar New Testament Commentary. Grand Rapids, MI: Eerdmans, 2012.
Lamb, David T. *The Emotions of God: Making Sense of a God Who Hates, Weeps, and Loves*. Downers Grove, IL: InterVarsity, 2022.
Linguee.com. "心有餘而力不足—English Translation." https://www.linguee.com/chinese-english/translation/%E5%BF%83%E6%9C%89%E9%A4%98%E8%80%8C%E5%8A%9B%E4%B8%8D%E8%B6%B3.html.
Longenecker, Richard N. *Galatians*. Word Biblical Commentary 41. Dallas: Word, 1990.
Millar, J. Gary. *Calling on the Name of the Lord: A Biblical Theology of Prayer*. New Studies in Biblical Theology. Downers Grove, IL: InterVarsity, 2016.
Morris, Leon. *The Gospel according to Matthew*. Pillar New Testament Commentary. Grand Rapids, MI: Eerdmans, 1992.
Nolland, John. *The Gospel of Matthew*. New International Greek Testament Commentary. Grand Rapids, MI: Eerdmans, 2005.
Osborne, Grant R. *Matthew*. Zondervan Exegetical Commentary on the New Testament. Grand Rapids, MI: Zondervan, 2010.
Oswalt, John N. "Holiness: God's Goal for Human Life." *Journal of the Evangelical Theological Society* 66.2 (June 2023) 267–78.
Schreiner, Thomas R. *Romans*. 2nd ed. Baker Exegetical Commentary on the New Testament. Grand Rapids, MI: Baker, 2018.
Tie, Peter L. H. "Spirit, Scripture, Saints, and Seminary: Toward a Reappropriation of 'Spirit Illumination' in 'Scripture Interpretation' for Seminarians." In *Spirit Wind: The Doctrine of the Holy Spirit in Global Theology—A Chinese Perspective*, edited by Peter L. H. Tie and Justin T. T. Tan, 3–36. Eugene, OR: Pickwick, 2021.
Turner, David L. *Matthew*. Baker Exegetical Commentary on the New Testament. Grand Rapids, MI: Baker Academic, 2008.
Wenk, Matthias. "Holy Spirit." In *Dictionary of Jesus and the Gospels*, edited by Joel B. Green, 387–94. 2nd ed. IVP Bible Dictionary Series. Downers Grove, IL: IVP Academic, 2013.

www.ingramcontent.com/pod-product-compliance
Lightning Source LLC
Chambersburg PA
CBHW050835160426
43192CB00010B/2031